Can We Recover the Original Text of the New Testament?

Can We Recover the Original Text of the New Testament?

Edited by

DAVID ALAN BLACK
& ABIDAN PAUL SHAH

Foreword by William F. Warren

WIPF & STOCK · Eugene, Oregon

CAN WE RECOVER THE ORIGINAL TEXT OF THE NEW
TESTAMENT?

Wipf & Stock
An Imprint of Wipf and Stock Publishers
199 W. 8th Ave., Suite 3
Eugene, OR 97401

www.wipfandstock.com

PAPERBACK ISBN: 978-1-6667-7374-3
HARDCOVER ISBN: 978-1-6667-7375-0
EBOOK ISBN: 978-1-6667-7376-7

VERSION NUMBER 10/16/23

Dedication:
To all those we have taught through the years from lectern and pulpit. May your continued study of the word of God lead you ever more directly to the One who is the way, the truth, and the life.

Contents

ACKNOWLEDGEMENTS

The editors wish to thank the Clearview staff, especially Ryan Hill, John Galantis, David Williamson, and Nicholas Shah, who worked very hard in the planning of the Clearview Apologetics Conference 2022.

CONTRIBUTORS

David Alan Black (D. Theol., University of Basel) has been teaching New Testament and Greek for 47 years, most recently at Southeastern Baptist Theological Seminary in Wake Forest, NC. An avid surfer, marathoner, and triathlete, he lives and works on a 123-acre farm in southern Virginia. He has authored or edited over 30 books, including *The Jesus Paradigm*, *New Testament Textual Criticism*, and *Learn to Read New Testament Greek*.

Peter J. Gurry (Ph.D., University of Cambridge) has been Associate Professor of New Testament at Phoenix Seminary since 2017 and is currently the Codirector of the Text & Canon Institute. He is the coauthor *of Scribes and Scripture: The Amazing Story of How We Got the Bible* and coeditor of *Myths and Mistakes in New Testament Textual Criticism*. He and his wife have six children. Peter is also a pastor at Whitton Avenue Bible Church in Phoenix.

Maurice A. Robinson (Ph.D., Southwestern Baptist Theological Seminary) is a retired professor who has been studying and working with NTTC for more than 50 years. His publications include *The New Testament in the Original Greek: Byzantine Textform 2005* (with William Pierpont). Maurice has examined more than 1750 continuous-text manuscripts and completely collated 1500 manuscripts and 500 lectionaries which relate to the *Pericope Adulterae* (John 7:53–8:11).

Abidan Paul Shah (Ph.D., Southeastern Baptist Theological Seminary) teaches New Testament and Greek at Carolina University, Winston Salem, and is the author of *Changing the Goalpost of New*

Testament Textual Criticism. He also has been serving as the senior pastor of Clearview Church in North Carolina for over 23 years where he lives with his beautiful wife and four children. Abidan is also the host of the daily talk radio show, *Clearview Today with Abidan Shah.*

William F. Warren (Ph.D., New Orleans Baptist Theological Seminary) is a professor of New Testament and Greek at New Orleans Baptist Theological Seminary and the founding director of H. Milton Haggard Center for New Testament Textual Studies. With over 40 years of ministry experience, he serves as a pastor, missionary, and church starter. He also serves on the Steering Committee of the International Greek New Testament Project.

FOREWORD

Books that let people explain their own viewpoints are help-ful, knowing that this approach provides a greater opportunity for accuracy in the expression of viewpoints and can help avoid overly simplistic if not unfair caricatures that those with opposing viewpoints might present. In this respect, this work allows for the three "viewpoint" writers to explain their own approach to New Testament textual criticism and to highlight what they see as the strengths of their particular methodology and approach versus what others might propose.

David Alan Black advocates the textual methodology of Harry Sturz as one that can be distinguished from the other approaches, and especially so versus the Byzantine or majority text methodologies. Black characterizes Sturz as having an approach that seeks to walk the line in respecting the three traditional textual streams, meaning those traditionally identified as Alexandrian, Western, and Byzantine groups. According to Black, this "middle-road" approach gives more credence to the Byzantine textual stream, while not moving into a "de facto" stance that would consistently favor that camp.

Maurice Robinson is in many ways the current "dean" of the majority text perspective, having written and presented in multiple contexts over several decades on his view that favors the Byzantine or majority text. He is also one of the editors along with William Pierpont of "The New Testament in the Original Greek: Byzantine Textform, 2005." Robinson presents the logic behind his methodology especially by way of numerous examples from the Greek text where variant readings are interpreted from his standpoint.

Peter Gurry is a younger scholar who is well-known in the mainstream settings of New Testament textual criticism where the reasoned eclecticism approach dominates. He is also acquainted with more recent methodological advances in the field, such as the coherence-based genealogical method, having co-authored a book on that method with Tommy Wasserman (*A New Approach to New Testament Textual Criticism: An Introduction to the Coherence-Based Genealogical Method*, 2017). Gurry seeks to show why the reasoned eclectic approach is superior to both the thorough-going eclectic approach and the majority text approach because of considering both the external manuscript witnesses and the internal scribal and authorial practices.

No matter what one's viewpoint about the best methodology for New Testament textual criticism, this book helps in the discussion by hearing from proponents with different viewpoints. Not that all will agree with the viewpoints (indeed, I differ substantially with some of the viewpoints), but hearing others is important for learning and dialogue. This book helps on that count with overall understandable explanations of detailed and involved issues.

Chapter 1

The Current Debate Over the Original Text of the New Testament

Abidan Paul Shah

In recent decades, the traditional definition of the original text of the New Testament (NT) has shifted from seeking one singular text to seeking a number of texts. Instead of one "authorial" text, now it is claimed that it could be one of several different texts based on their locations in the history of transmission: preauthorial, authorial, canonical, and postcanonical. These distinctions were first listed by Eldon Epp in his article "The Multivalence of the Term 'Original Text' in New Testament Textual Criticism" as "predecessor," "autographic," "canonical," and "interpretive" text-forms.[1] He defined the new "legitimate sphere" of NT Textual Criticism as follows:

> Any search for textual *pre*formulations or *re*formulations of a literary nature, such as *prior* compositional levels, versions, or formulations, or *later* textual alteration, revision, division, combination, rearrangement, interpolation, or forming a collection of writings, legitimately

1. Epp, "Multivalence," 276–77.

> falls within the sphere of text-critical activity *if such an exploration is initiated on the basis of some appropriate textual variation or other manuscript evidence.*[2]

Following on the heels of the new shift, and even concurrently, has been the advent of the Coherence-Based Genealogical Method (CBGM) with a yet-new taxonomy—authorial text, *Ausgangstext* or "initial" text, and archetypal text.[3] Authorial text retains the traditional definition of the original text. *Ausgangstext* is defined by its progenitor Gerd Mink as "a hypothetical, reconstructed text, as it presumably existed, according to the hypothesis, before the beginning of its copying."[4] To clarify, it does not exist in any manuscript but has to be created piecemeal from the extant manuscript evidence. The third category of the archetypal text is the starting point of the family tree which gave rise to all the extant manuscripts. According to CBGM proponents, this text should not be the ultimate goal since the surviving witnesses can be flawed. In such a case, efforts must be made to restore the initial text, a text that is prior to the period of the entrance of any errors, albeit a hypothetical ancestor. This could be the authorial text but has to be so proven. Klaus Wachtel further elaborates:

> [T]he definition of the term 'initial text' must be carefully distinguished from the archetype of the tradition, on the one hand, and from the original text of the author, on the other. The archetype of the tradition was a real manuscript, the copy by which the transmission started

---

2. Epp, "Multivalence," 268 (emphasis original). The first three categories of "predecessor," "autographic," and "canonical" text-forms are the byproducts of the conclusions of form criticism, source criticism, redaction criticism, and canonical criticism. Epp's final category of "interpretive" text-form may be coming from the new trend in NTTC of placing undue emphasis on scribal variants.

3. Wachtel and Holmes, "Introduction," 7. Also see Mink, "Problems," 25–27. Gurry, one of the contributors to this volume, under his text-critical methodology, gives a positive assessment to the term "initial text" by identifying it as possibly the authorial text and no threat to inerrancy. See Gurry, "Inerrancy and the Initial Text," 54-67.

4. Mink, "Problems," 25.

that put forth the manuscripts we have—and many more that are lost. The original text of the author predates the manuscripts we have by more than a century in most cases. The initial text is the hypothetical reconstruction of the text as it was before the archetype of the tradition emerged. The initial text is the result of methodical efforts to approximate most closely the lost text of the author based on all relevant evidence, not excluding any trace of transmission predating the archetype.[5]

In his comprehensive article "From 'Original Text' to 'Initial Text,'" Michael Holmes, still a proponent of the traditional quest of the original text, gave a favorable yet cautious assessment of the CBGM shift in nomenclature of the original text:

> The concept of the initial text is both empirically grounded, in that it seeks to determine the textual form(s) (archetypes) from which the extant evidence derives, and also theoretically open-ended, in that it both seeks to move beyond the archetype(s) to the initial text, and leaves open the question of the relationship between the initial text and any earlier form(s) of text. Thus it is able to serve the interests and purposes of a variety of perspectives and approaches, including those who may wish to recover no more that the earliest surviving text(s), those who wish to focus on the history of the transmission and reception of these text(s), and those who may wish to investigate the relationship between the initial text and the origin(s) of the textual tradition of which it is a part. It remains to be seen, of course, whether and how widely the *Ausgangstext* will become accepted as the basic goal of the discipline; that is, however, its potential.[6]

It is apparent that with such changing definitions of the original text of the NT, text-critics are ambivalent about reaching the traditional goal of NT textual criticism. Instead, attention is now given towards hypothesizing regarding the emergence of the variant readings. Furthermore, any attempt towards utilizing

5. Taken from Wachtel, "Conclusion," 219

6. Holmes, "'Original Text' to 'Initial Text,'" 680–81.

text-critical principles to reach the original text is looked upon as being out of date and pointless. Moreover, proponents of the new movement place the blame for the traditional goal of NT textual criticism of retrieving the original text upon either the printing press or the Reformation.[7] They claim that the idea of an errorless original was nonexistent prior to the printing press. Also, they blame the lack of *ex cathedra* teaching of the Roman Catholic Church as the impetus for the Scripture becoming errorless and authoritative. It is even claimed that the idea of the "original text" is historically indefensible considering historical-critical conclusions, reception of the writings by the early church, and the state of the text after the first couple of hundred years of Christianity.

NEW DEFINITIONS OF THE ORIGINAL TEXT OF THE NEW TESTAMENT

PREAUTHORIAL TEXT	AUTHORIAL TEXT
AUTHORIAL TEXT	AUSGANGSTEXT/ INITIAL TEXT
CANONICAL TEXT	
POSTCANONICAL TEXT	ARCHETYPAL TEXT

All such shifting definitions of the original text and the ensuing claims have far-reaching consequences for biblical faith and praxis. As I have written elsewhere, "Without a generally definitive text, the door will be left wide open to recreate any desired text of the NT. An unsettled original text will result in an unsettled biblical theology due to a lack of any authoritative and standard text. Consequently, it will lead to an unsettled Christian faith and practice."[8] Furthermore, this challenge against the traditional quest for the

---

7. Parker, *Living Text*, 212. Similar suggestions are also made by Knust, "In Pursuit," 188 and Holmes, "'Original Text' to 'Initial Text,'" 642.

8. Shah, *Changing the Goalpost*, 8.

original text cannot be treated with indolence. The recent influx of writings promoting the abandonment of the original quest and the no-holds-barred challenge from Bart Ehrman (professor at UNC Chapel Hill and admitted agnostic) demand an answer. In his best-seller *Misquoting Jesus*, he characteristically challenged those who think they have the original text and thus believe in the doctrine of inerrancy in the following words:

> [H]ow does it help us to say that the Bible is the inerrant word of God if in fact we don't have the words that God inerrantly inspired, but only the words copied by the scribes—sometimes correctly but sometimes (many times!) incorrectly? What good is it to say that the autographs (i.e., the originals) were inspired? We don't have the originals! We have only error-ridden copies, and the vast majority of these are centuries removed from the originals and different from them, evidently, in thousands of ways.[9]

Is Ehrman accurate regarding his claim? Is the text of the NT too far gone to be ever reclaimed? To begin with, there are four allegations that Ehrman makes against the integrity of the NT text: "We don't have the originals!" "We have only error-ridden copies," "the vast majority of these are centuries removed from the originals," and "different from them, evidently, in thousands of ways." Before each of the allegations listed above are tackled, Ehrman's misunderstanding of the doctrine of inerrancy should be first addressed.

Systematic theologian Millard Erickson explains: "[Inerrancy] is a corollary of the doctrine of full inspiration of the Bible. The view of the Bible held and taught by the writers of Scripture implies the full truthfulness of the Bible."[10] Greg Bahnsen also clarifies that:

---

9. Ehrman, *Misquoting* Jesus, 7. In a recent post at the Evangelical Textual Criticism blog, Peter Gurry discussed Ehrman's definition of textual criticism, which is far more traditional than his sensational comments in his popular *Misquoting Jesus*. See Gurry, "Ehrman's Definition."

10. Erickson, *Christian Theology*, 255.

> It is not a doctrine derived from empirical investigation
> of certain written texts; it is a theological commitment
> rooted in the teaching of the Word of God itself. The
> nature of God (who is truth Himself) and the nature of
> the biblical books (as the very words of God) require that
> we view the original manuscripts, produced under the
> superintendence of the Holy Spirit of truth, as wholly
> true and without error.[11]

In other words, the basis of inerrancy is inspiration. Paul affirms the latter in 2 Tim 3:16, "All Scripture is given by inspiration of God."[12] Inspiration comes from the Greek adjective θεόπνευστος *(theopneustos)*, literally "God-breathed." More specifically, all the words, including the whole message, is the breath of God. This is referred to as the verbal-plenary view of inspiration. As to the actual workings of this view, God directed the thoughts of the writers so that they were exactly his thoughts. He used the personalities, gifts, trainings, and experiences of the writers, but the final choice of the words was exactly what he wanted in his providential guidance in the writer's life and God's purposes in the world. As Peter explains in 2 Pet 1:21, "for prophecy never came by the will of man, but holy men of God spoke as they were moved by the Holy Spirit." The Greek word for "move" is ʼφέρω *(phero)*, which means "lead, guide, and carry along." This model of inspiration is sometimes referred to as the "Incarnational Model of Scripture."[13] Just as Jesus had both the divine and human natures but remained sinless, so also Scripture is both divine and human but theoretically considered to be without any errors. In 1 Thess 2:13, Paul alludes interchangeably to the divine and human elements of Scripture: "For this reason we also thank God without ceasing, because when you received the word of God which you heard from us, you welcomed it not as the word of men, but as it

11. Bahnsen, "Inerrancy of the Autographa," 189.

12. All Scriptures are taken from the NKJV.

13. Mohler, "When the Bible speaks," 126. In this same book, Peter Enns also affirms an incarnational model of Scripture but his understanding of the human element allows for mistakes and errors.

is in truth, the word of God, which also effectively works in you who believe." It appears that the first writers and the early church understood that the words of the Scripture (OT as well as NT) were God's words, albeit written by the apostles or close associates of the apostles. Being God's words, they were truthful since God is truthful. Consider the following sample of references that testify to the truthfulness of God.

- Num 23:19: "God is not a man, that he should lie, nor a son of man, that he should repent. Has he said, and will he not do? Or has he spoken, and will he not make it good?"

- Ps 119:160: "The entirety of your word is truth, and every one of your righteous judgments endures forever."

- Matt 5:18: "For assuredly, I say to you, till heaven and earth pass away, one jot or one tittle will by no means pass from the law till all is fulfilled."

- John 17:17: "Sanctify them by your truth. Your word is truth."

- Titus 1:2: ". . . in hope of eternal life which God, who cannot lie, promised before time began."

Hence, if God is truthful, it logically follows that his word is truthful and consequently inerrant. Inerrancy is thus defined as, "when all the facts are known, the Scriptures in their original autographs and properly interpreted will be shown to be wholly true in everything that they affirm, whether that has to do with doctrine or morality or with the social, physical, or life sciences."[14]

Furthermore, inerrancy does not serve textual criticism. To the contrary, textual criticism finds its legitimacy as a discipline due to inerrancy. J. I. Packer explains:

> Text criticism serves inerrancy; they are friends. Inerrancy treasures the meaning of each writer's words, while text criticism checks that we have each writer's words

14. Feinberg, "Meaning of Inerrancy," 294. To clarify, it is better to use inerrancy rather than infallibility because the latter is usually used by those who allow for the possibility that the Bible may not be fully free from error. They limit inerrancy to matters of faith and practice, especially salvation.

pure and intact. Both these wisdoms are needed if we are
to benefit fully from the written Word of God.[15]

Although the new wave in NT textual criticism is focused
on using the discipline as a window on the history of the church,
its true and proper use has always been to retrieve the inerrant
original text.

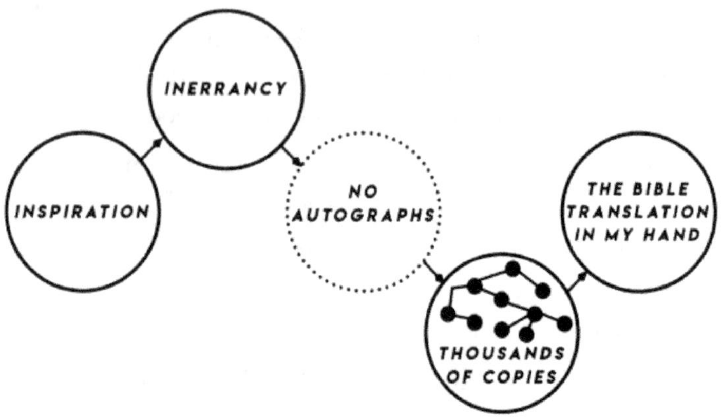

Having established that the doctrine of inerrancy is not up
for debate, let us focus on the four allegations of Ehrman.

1. *"WE DON'T HAVE THE ORIGINALS!"*

Ehrman is correct. We do not have the autographs. This sometimes comes as a shock to some that we do not have the original
documents on which Matthew, Mark, Luke, John, Paul, or the rest
of the NT writers wrote, but this should be understandable. After
all, it has been almost two thousand years since the NT was first
written! More than likely, the first documents were written on pa-
pyrus, which is a plant that was primarily found in Egypt around
the Nile delta—not the most durable material. Furthermore, the
humid climate around the Mediterranean Sea made it difficult for
such a material to last a long time. Nonetheless, it is not a matter of

---

15. Packer, "Text Criticism and Inerrancy," 102.

angst, because it is not the first documents that were inspired but simply the words on them. It is often assumed that once a document was lost, the text was lost with it. Such is obviously not true since there are numerous copies scattered around, albeit there are variants among the manuscripts. Imagine the first document to be the meter stick at the Smithsonian. If it were to be stolen, how would that impact our understanding of a meter? It really would not. There are plenty of meter sticks from various manufacturers and time periods lying around. All we must do is to put a sample together, and we can easily determine the average meter.[16] The way Ehrman makes it sound, since we do not have the original meter stick, we can no longer know for sure if the meter was one millimeter, one centimeter, or one meter. Such is far from the case. The answer to the second allegation will clarify the nature and extent of the corruption.

2. *"WE HAVE ONLY ERROR-RIDDEN COPIES."*

Ehrman is correct again. The scribes did make mistakes in their copying. A simple attempt at copying a single page by hand will easily convince anyone of how easy it is to make scribal mistakes. Basically, they made two kinds of mistakes:

- Unintentional (faulty eyesight, faulty hearing, errors of the mind, errors of judgment)

- Intentional (spelling and grammar, harmonizing, explaining history and geography, doctrinal—very few)

However, it is totally misleading to claim that the copies are "error-ridden." Ehrman even tries to give a count of these mistakes with his often-repeated statement—"with only 138,000 words in the NT, there are as many as 400,000 or more variants in the NT manuscript tradition."[17] Such claims and counts are misleading at

---

16. This scenario is adapted from R. L. Harris's work on inspiration. See Harris, *Inspiration and Canonicity*, 88–89.

17 Ehrman, *Misquoting Jesus*, 89.

best and only serve to shock those who are unaware. In reality, all such numbers are just estimations. Also, most of the mistakes in the NT manuscripts are unintentional and insignificant.[18] Overall, approximately 94 percent of the text is totally reliable. It is only the remaining 5–6 percent that is in question. Most text-critics on both sides of the aisle agree that the NT text confirms "Macro Stability and Micro Fluidity."[19] Several studies have proven that the NT text is incredibly stable, even in the period of the earliest papyri when most of the variants entered the transmissional history. Maurice A. Robinson's paper, "The Integrity of the Early New Testament Text: A Collation-Based Comparison Utilizing the Papyri of the Second and Third Centuries," shows the papyri remained stable over 90 percent of the time.[20] So also the works of Barbara Aland on P45, P46, P66, and P75 and Kim Haines-Eitzen's *Guardians of Letters: Literacy, Power, and the Transmitters of Early Christian Literature* prove the overall stabilityof the NT text in the early centuries.[21]

Given the multitude of the manuscripts and relative insignificance of the remaining variants, in most instances there is no problem in retrieving the original text. Oddly enough, Ehrman affirms this as well: "By far the vast majority [of variants] are purely 'accidental,' readily explained as resulting from scribal ineptitude, carelessness, or fatigue."[22] Nonetheless, in practice, Ehrman portrays the intentional changes as far more prevalent and irreparable.

18. Gurry, "Number of Variants," 97–121. Also see Gurry's essay, "Myths About Variants," 191–210.

19. Holmes, "Text and Transmission," 78.

20. Robinson, "Integrity," 1–24.

21. Aland, "Kriterien," 1–13; Aland, "Der textkritische," 19–38; Aland, "Significance," 108–21; and Aland, "Textual Research," 13–26. Also see, Haines-Eitzen, *Guardians*, 106.

22. Ehrman, *Orthodox Corruption*, 31.

3. *"THE VAST MAJORITY OF THESE ARE CENTURIES REMOVED FROM THE ORIGINALS," AND "DIFFERENT FROM THEM, EVIDENTLY, IN THOUSANDS OF WAYS."*

Ehrman is yet correct again. The earliest copies are several centuries removed from the originals. In fact, much of the debate in NT textual criticism is because of this early gap in the manuscript evidence, but that is not as much a problem as Ehrman makes it out to be. There are three things to keep in mind when thinking about the NT text in these early centuries:

A. Authors' Self Awareness

With the coming of the Enlightenment in the eighteenth century and the rise of historical criticism, it is assumed that the authors were unaware that their writings were the Word of God, the Holy Scripture on the same level as the Old Testament (OT). Harry Gamble in his book *The New Testament Canon: Its Making and Meaning*, writes, "None of the writings which belong to the NT was composed as scripture…(They) were written for immediate and practical purposes within the early churches, and only gradually did they come to be valued and to be spoken of as 'scripture.'"[23] So also, D. Moody Smith in his presidential address at the 1999 SBL Annual Meeting opened with the words:

> In teaching NT Introduction, I am fond of saying that the authors of NT books would have had no inkling that their writings would become part of something called the New Testament or the Christian Bible, which did not reach exactly its present form until the fourth century. Matthew did not know that his Gospel would begin the NT, although he would be happy to discover that it does. It is well suited for that position and purpose. John did not know that his Gospel would stand in the

---

23. Gamble, *New Testament Canon*, 18.

NT alongside three other, Synoptic Gospels, and that it would be the fourth, presumably to be read after the others.[24]

Scot McKnight, in his book *The Blue Parakeet: Rethinking How You Read the Bible*, recalls a time when F. F. Bruce remarked, "I think Paul would roll over in his grave if he knew we were turning his letters into *torah*."[25]

Were the authors of the NT truly unaware that they were writing Scripture? I don't think that they were aware to the extent of knowing that what they were writing was going to be part of a twenty-seven-book collection called the NT, but they seemed to be acutely aware that what they were writing was under the special influence of the Holy Spirit and was going to be used by the people of God as their authoritative guide for salvation and everyday life on the same level as the OT Scripture. The NT writings give plenty of evidence that prove this—2 Tim 3:16, "All Scripture is given by inspiration of God;" 2 Pet 1:21, "Holy men of God spoke as they were moved by the Holy Spirit;" 1 Thess 2:13, "You received the word of God which you heard from us, you welcomed it not as the word of men, but as it is in truth, the word of God;" and 1 Cor 14:37, "If anyone thinks himself to be a prophet or spiritual, let him acknowledge that the things which I write to you are the commandments of the Lord." The above references give compelling indication that the apostles were aware of the special nature of their writings.

Moreover, we have a couple of proofs in the NT itself that testify to the NT writings being referred to as "Scripture" very early on. 1 Timothy 5:17–18: "Let the elders who rule well be counted worthy of double honor, especially those who labor in the word and doctrine. For the Scripture says, 'You shall not muzzle an ox while it treads out the grain,' and, 'The laborer is worthy of his wages.'" Here, Paul uses two references for "Scripture," the first from Deut 25:4 and the second from Luke 10:7. This implies that the gospel of Luke was being treated as "Scripture" on the same level as the

24. Smith, "When Did the Gospels," 3.

25. McKnight, *Blue Parakeet*, 207.

OT writings. Also, in 2 Pet 3:15–16: "... and consider that the longsuffering of our Lord is salvation—as also our beloved brother Paul, according to the wisdom given to him, has written to you, as also in all his epistles, speaking in them of these things, in which are some things hard to understand, which untaught and unstable people twist to their own destruction, as they do also the rest of the Scriptures." Three important deductions can be made here: First, at least some of Paul's letters were already traveling together as a possible unit; second, they were being treated on the same level as Scripture (in this context, OT writings); and thirdly, they were being twisted by those who were "untaught" and "untrained." Peter's remark demonstrates an effort to safeguard the NT writings while they were being written or shortly after. According to church tradition, both Peter and Paul were martyred under the evil Roman emperor Nero (before AD 68). This means that the NT writings were being held up as God's Word on the same status as the OT writings before AD 70, that's thirty years after Jesus ascended. This could also be evidence for an early canon, which is beyond the scope of this discussion.[26]

Corroborative evidence supporting the author's self-awareness can also be noted in the content and tone of the introductions of the gospels and the epistles. The beginning of each gospel gives the sense that it is a continuation of the OT Scripture. Matthew 1:1–2: "The book of the genealogy of Jesus Christ, the Son of David, the Son of Abraham: Abraham begot Isaac, Isaac begot Jacob, and Jacob begot Judah and his brothers." In other words, the gospel was grounded in the story of God's people, going back to their great King David and even past him to the patriarchs, Abraham, Isaac, and Jacob. Mark 1:1–3: "The beginning of the gospel of Jesus Christ, the Son of God. As it is written in the Prophets: 'Behold, I send My messenger before your face, who will prepare your way before you.' 'The voice of one crying in the wilderness: 'Prepare the

---

26. The concept of non-Pauline and non-Petrine "forgeries" or "pseude-pigrapha" is rejected by most evangelicals, although promoted by Ehrman and held by most non-evangelical and liberal scholars. See chapters 2 and 3 of Ehrman, *Forged.*

way of the Lord; Make his paths straight."' Mark begins by quoting from Mal 3:1 and Isa 40:3, two prominent prophets of the Jewish people. In a sense, Mark is legitimizing his account by presenting it as a fulfillment of Malachi and Isaiah.

Luke gives a lengthy preamble that not only lays out his research methodology but also introduces his writing as a "fulfillment" of OT prophecies. Luke 1:1–4: "Inasmuch as many have taken in hand to set in order a narrative of those things which have been fulfilled among us, just as those who from the beginning were eyewitnesses and ministers of the word delivered[27] them to us, it seemed good to me also, having had perfect understanding of all things from the very first, to write to you an orderly account, most excellent Theophilus, that you may know the certainty of those things in which you were instructed." Finally, John's opening lines clearly reveal that a new beginning had happened with the coming of Jesus. John 1:1: "In the beginning was the Word, and the Word was with God, and the Word was God." One cannot help but recall Gen 1:1: "In the beginning God created the heavens and the earth." The gospel writers were not only aware of the inspiration through the Holy Spirit, but they also seem to be aware that they were completing Israel's story, the OT Scripture.

This can also be said about the rest of the NT writings. Case in point is Paul's introduction to his letter to the Romans. Romans 1:1–4: "Paul, a bondservant of Jesus Christ, called to be an apostle, separated to the gospel of God which he promised before through his prophets in the Holy Scriptures, concerning his Son Jesus Christ our Lord, who was born of the seed of David according to the flesh, and declared to be the Son of God with power according to the Spirit of holiness, by the resurrection from the dead." So also, Peter opens his first epistle as follows: 1 Pet 1:1: "Peter, an apostle of Jesus Christ, to the pilgrims of the Dispersion in Pontus, Galatia, Cappadocia, Asia, and Bithynia . . ." It is obvious that Peter was writing to encourage believers of Jewish background who were scattered all over the known world. The point of this discussion is

---

27 Here παραδίδωμι (*paradidomi*) refers to the apostolic handing down of the authoritative tradition.

that the NT writers were not only aware that they were writing Holy Scripture, but they were also cognizant of the fact that they were continuing the story of the OT.

Overall, scribes would have been hesitant to tamper with writings that were deemed Holy Spirit inspired by the original writers, referred to as Scripture by fellow apostles, and seen as fulfilling and continuing the OT Scripture by the apostles. If they were tempted to introduce any malicious error, there was strict warning in Rev 22:18–19: "For I testify to everyone who hears the words of the prophecy of this book: If anyone adds to these things, God will add to him the plagues that are written in this book; and if anyone takes away from the words of the book of this prophecy, God shall take away his part from the Book of Life, from the holy city, and from the things which are written in this book."

B. Reception by the Early Church

Consider the following statements by:

- Tischendorf: "I have no doubt that in the very earliest ages after our Holy Scriptures were written, and before the authority of the Church protected them, willful alterations, and especially additions, were made in them."[28]

- Scrivener: "It is no less true to fact than paradoxical in sound, that the worst corruptions to which the New Testament has ever been subjected, originated within a hundred years after it was composed."[29]

- Zuntz: "Modern criticism stops before the barrier of the second century; the age, so it seems, of unbounded liberties with the text."[30]

---

28. Tischendorf, *New Testament*, xv.

29. Scrivener, *Plain Introduction*, 2:264.

30. Zuntz, *Text of the Epistles*, 11.

Even so, there is plenty of evidence from early church history of efforts at preserving the original text of the NT. Origen, in his work *Against Celsus*, observed:

> Now I know of no others who have altered the Gospel, save the followers of Marcion, and those of Valentinus, and, I think, also those of Lucian. But such an allegation is no charge against the Christian system, but against those who dared so to trifle with the Gospels.[31]

Eusebius, church father and historian, gives several important testimonies regarding the awareness of the attempt by some to corrupt the text of the NT. He quotes from Gaius:

> For this reason is it they have boldly laid their hands upon the divine Scriptures, alleging that they have corrected them. And that I do not state this against them falsely, any one who pleases may ascertain. For if any one should choose to collect and compare all their copies together, he would find many discrepancies among them.[32]

Eusebius also quotes from Dionysius of Corinth regarding the attempt of the heretics to corrupt both his own letter and Scripture.[33] Irenaeus strictly warned those who would copy his writings to exercise caution.[34] Given such strict warnings against corruption in extrabiblical writings, one can only imagine the care that would be taken in copying the holy writings.

Furthermore, there is evidence that very early on, the church deemed canonical those works that became part of the NT canon. Among other factors, the public reading of Scripture in the early church, with special authority to the lectors, and the numerous

31. Origen, *Against Celsus*, 2.27. For English translation, see Roberts, Donaldson, and Coxe, *Ante-Nicene Fathers*, 4:443.

32. Eusebius, *Ecclesiastical History*, 5.28. English translation taken from Roberts, Donaldson, and Coxe, *Ante-Nicene Fathers*, 5:602.

33. Eusebius, *Ecclesiastical History*, 4.23. See Cruse, trans., *Eusebius' Ecclesiastical History*, 135–36.

34. Irenaeus, *On the Ogdoad* (no longer extant), as reported by Eusebius in *Ecclesiastical History* 5.20.2 as found in Metzger and Ehrman, *Text of the New Testament*, 33.

allusions by the early church fathers to the NT books are strong evidence of early canonicity.[35] It is mistakenly assumed that the books were deemed canonical at the councils in the fourth century. Peter Balla, in his article "Evidence for an Early Christian Canon (Second and Third Century)," counters:

> The fact that church councils only made decisions in the latter part of the fourth century can be evaluated in two ways. It may bear witness to the creation of the canon at that time; however, it can also be argued that there was no need of decisions in the preceding centuries, because the "canonical process" was well on its way. Perhaps the situation in the fourth century—for example, in the time of Eusebius—differed so greatly from that of earlier centuries that it is not a good starting point for a reconstruction of the history of the canon.[36]

The early church's reception of the NT books and hints of early informal canonization points to a high regard for the text of the NT and less propensity towards careless corruption of the NT text.

C. Ancient Book Production

In recent years, research from Greco-Roman book production is used to challenge traditional understanding of the original text of the NT. A representative example is Matthew Larsen's *Gospels Before the Book*. He begins his preface with "This is a book about unfinishedness and unfinalizability."[37] In his article, "Accidental Publication, Unfinished Texts and the Traditional Goals of New Testament Textual Criticism," he claims that textual unfinishedness, accidental publications, post-publication revisions, and multiple authorized versions of the same work were a normal part of book production.[38] Such claims are based on the assumptions that there are no authorial, original, or final text of the NT books.

35. Balla, "Evidence," 372–85.
36. Balla, "Evidence," 384.
37. Larsen, *Gospels Before the Book*, xiii.
38. Larsen, "Accidental Publication," 362–87.

Timothy Mitchell has countered Larsen's claim by demonstrating through a survey of Greco-Roman literary world that "[t]he text was fluid in some respects . . . but the authors (in this case Martial, Quintilian, Galen, and Octavius) clearly distinguished between these altered texts and their initially released versions."[39]

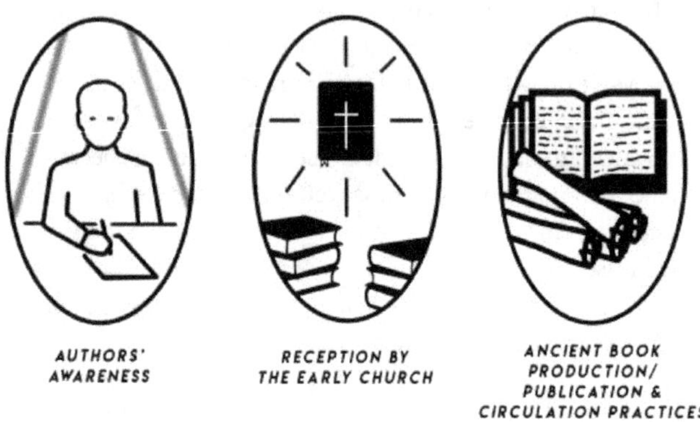

CONCLUSION

Contrary to what Ehrman has alleged, scribes were not as careless or prone to intentional alteration as they are made out to be. They had different levels of skills and abilities. Overall, they operated from a perspective that they were handling the word of God, similar to the intent of the original writers. Corrections were made before finishing a manuscript or by later scribes. Overall, the core textual tradition is stable. No doctrine is in jeopardy. Most errors were early, but generally explainable. Very few would be doctrinally significant. It is imperative that we determine the original words of the NT because these are the actual words of God. Harold Greenlee, famous text-critic of yesteryear, wrote:

> The reason for studying the manuscripts, then, is not
> to decide whether the New Testament does or does not
> teach certain basic truths but rather, for the most part,
> to decide small details and relatively minor matters.

39. Mitchell, "Myths about Autographs," 26–47.

> Someone might ask, then, why we should bother at all if no important truths are at stake. The answer is that the New Testament is of such supreme importance that if careful study will enable us to make our text even slightly closer to what the New Testament writers wrote, or if it will enable us to see that our New Testament is already as nearly identical with the original text as it can be made, it will be worth the effort.[40]

In the following chapters, three different scholars will present their methodologies for retrieving the original text of the NT. This was the intent of the 2022 Clearview Apologetics Conference on the original text of the NT. Each of them represents a particular methodology regarding NT textual criticism. Each methodology evaluates the manuscript evidence differently. The evidence can be divided into two categories: internal and external. Internal evidence deals with what the scribe or scribes might have done at a particular point in the text, intentionally or unintentionally. Its basic principle is, "The reading from which the other readings could most easily have developed is most likely the original."[41] This is followed by other principles regarding harder and shorter readings, author's style, vocabulary, syntax, themes, and other matters. External evidence deals with the various manuscripts and other witnesses in deciding which reading is best supported. These include papyri, uncials, minuscules, lectionaries, versions (Latin, Syriac, Coptic), patristic quotations, etc. This is where we come across text-types, or textual "clusters," such as the Alexandrian, Byzantine, Western, and maybe even Caesarean. We have a lot of evidence, somewhere around five thousand and one hundred Greek manuscripts plus tens of thousands of the other witnesses, but we need to be careful in how we use that number. No matter how each of the presenters evaluates the text-critical evidence, it is obvious that they all believe in the inerrancy and retrievability of the NT text

---

40. Greenlee, *Text of the New Testament*, 58–59.

41. Greenlee, *Text of the New Testament*, 59.

Chapter 2

REASONED ECLECTICISM AND THE ORIGINAL TEXT

PETER J. GURRY

THE TEXT OF THE New Testament is one of the best attested sets of works from antiquity. It has come down to us in thousands of Greek manuscripts as well as hundreds more in other languages to say nothing of the citations from early Christian writers. The simple fact is that these manuscripts do not always agree with each other. If we want to know what the New Testament writers said, we need a way to decide which copies have gone wrong and where.

There are some who, for theological reasons, would prefer that no one today make such decisions. Instead, they argue that we ought to follow the trail of God's providence to the right text.[1] In practice, what this typically means is following someone else's decisions from the past, usually those made in the sixteenth and seventeenth centuries. But I am convinced that, because of the tremendous manuscript discoveries Providence has provided over the last one hundred and fifty years, we must continue to examine manuscripts and so make our decisions. To do otherwise would be a dereliction of a *Christian* duty. It would amount to a denial of

1. This approach goes by various names, but a representative version can be found in Hills, *King James Version Defended*.

God's providence beyond the seventeenth century. Thankfully, my fellow contributors all agree that decisions can and must be made today and so I will set aside any further justification for it.

Where we disagree is on precisely how to go about making those decisions. I say that we disagree on *precisely* how because my knowledge of the other men's work suggests that our agreement outweighs our disagreement. Even in results, the amount of overlap vastly outpaces the amount of disagreement. But textual criticism only exists because there is disagreement and so it naturally occupies the bulk of people's interest. The same is true methodologically. Apparently, no one wants to read an essay on all the ways we agree! So, the question remains about how I approach the question of resolving the differences between our New Testament manuscripts and how that differs from the other methods used today.

My own approach is what is known as reasoned eclecticism and it should be stated up front that this approach is the dominant one used by New Testament scholars over the last several hundred years. Today, it is often the main, or sometimes the only, method taught to students in seminary and the one most often used by commentators and Bible translators. I say this as a matter of fact not in order to brag or to prejudge the debate. Being the majority position, after all, does not make it right. In fact, there is some degree of danger that its majority status is the result of thinking with the crowd. Nevertheless, I do think it is right and that is, to the best of my own self-knowledge, why I hold it. I hope to explain why in what follows.

To do that, I would like to first explain what the method is, how it is distinct from other methods, and then finally why I think it offers a better approach than its competitors. But, first, a brief word on the history of the term.

BRIEF HISTORY OF THE TERM

For nearly a century, textual critics have used the term "eclectic" to describe their practice of textual criticism. But only more recently has the term been split into two types: reasoned and thoroughgoing.[2] To anticipate our later discussion, the key feature of reasoned eclecticism is that it tries to balance two types of evidence for which reading is original. The first is internal evidence and leverages what we know about scribal mistakes on the one hand and the author's own style or theology on the other. External evidence, in contrast, has to do with our knowledge of the various witnesses that attest each reading, especially their date, quality, geographical origin, and possible relationships to each other. Thoroughgoing eclecticism, on the other hand, focuses primarily on internal evidence.

The earliest reference I have found to the term "reasonable eclecticism" to describe textual criticism is in an 1884 edition of the Latin works of John Wycliffe edited by Rudolf Beers.[3] But Beers uses the term to designate his primary use of a single manuscript that he sometimes (eclectically) deviates from. More importantly, Beers is not working on the New Testament.

The first reference that scholars point to for the New Testament is in the title to the massive study by Marie-Joseph Lagrange, whose second volume is titled *La critique rationnelle*, that is, rational or reasoned criticism.[4] The best I can tell, Lagrange does advocate for something like today's reasoned eclecticism. He thinks the basic outlines of text-types can be discerned and that various criteria can be used to evaluate their quality.[5] These can then be used to help identify the original text. More important (because it is much clearer) is Leo Vaganay's discussion of method in his *Introduction* where he advocates for the "eclectic method." What is helpful in Vaganay's discussion is that he explicitly defines eclecticism as honoring both external and internal criteria. He says that

2. See the survey at the beginning of Epp, "Eclectic Method," 141–73.

3. Beers, *Ioannis Wyclif*, x

4. Lagrange, *Critique*. Metzger and Ehrman, *Text of the New Testament*, 222, put Lagrange under the heading of thoroughgoing eclecticism but their note that Lagrange pays more attention to external evidence "than one would have thought likely" betrays the fact that he does not belong there.

5. The basic method and the criteria for judging recensions are explained in Lagrange, *Critique*, 17–39.

there should be "no shutting up of the different branches of the science into watertight compartments."[6] This is in contrast to the situation of his day in which two schools dominated the editing of classical and medieval texts in France and Germany at the time.[7] Though we don't have space to elaborate, the differences between the German and French schools bear interesting similarities to New Testament methods to the degree that the Byzantine priority position is built on confidence in its ability to delineate textual history and thoroughgoing eclecticism is built on a pessimism about that same task.

Be that as it may, the most important development in the distinction between the two types of eclecticism in New Testament studies comes from G. D. Kilpatrick.[8] Kilpatrick praises the recent work of C. H. Turner because it was not hidebound to following one particular manuscript or text-type but was willing to use criteria that were "independent of any one text-type."[9] Kilpatrick approves of this approach but goes even further than Turner in having no preference for a given *manuscript* or text-type (whereas Turner still found Vaticanus to be the best in his particular study). Kilpatrick calls his version of eclecticism "rigorous" because "what is required is not a concession now and then to the eclectic method but the consistent application of that method…"[10] In this, he wants

6. Vaganay, *Introduction*, 91. I am indebted to Gordon Fee for pointing me to both Lagrange and Vaganay in his essay "Rigorous or Reasoned," 174–97; repr. in Epp and Fee, *Studies in the Theory*, 124–40.

7. Vaganay, *Introduction*, 91–92. The two schools were represented by Karl Lachmann on the one hand that made the relations of witnesses essential to textual criticism and that of Joseph Bédier on the other who made the editor's own judgment the key. For the historical background of these two schools, see Greetham, "History," 16–41 and the relevant chapters in Greetham, *Scholarly Editing*.

8. Kilpatrick, "Western Text," 32, referring to Turner, "Marcan Usage," 9–30.

9. Kilpatrick, "Western Text," 25.

10. Kilpatrick, "Western Text," 34.

to approach the question of the original text "in some independence of the problem of type," that is text-type.[11] He says:

> We may then conclude our inquiry by suggesting that the textual criteria require a rigorous eclecticism and indicate that, although the Alexandrian text and especially B are our best authorities, yet all the early types and witnesses contribute something of value, and none can be rejected.[12]

Despite Kilpatrick's qualification of "eclecticism" no one at the time distinguished two forms of it. By 1964, Bruce Metzger could still discuss Kilpatrick's view with the unqualified heading of "eclecticism" in what would become the standard introduction to the field.[13] That does not mean Metzger agrees with it. Instead, while admiring some of Kilpatrick's principles, he critiques it for being willing to follow readings that are too poorly attested (he lists twelve examples). Despite overlap, Kilpatrick's view is not Metzger's though Metzger gives no label to his own view. By the fourth edition in 2005, however, the preferred term for Kilpatrick's view has changed to "thoroughgoing eclecticism" and is presented in contrast to his own "reasoned eclecticism."[14] In those forty years, the two methods had become distinct.

In that time, it became increasingly clear that the term "eclecticism" was being used for approaches that diverged too much to share the same unqualified term.[15] Today, there is a third major approach that is usually set alongside these two known as Byzantine priority with roots going back earlier to Dean Burgon and F. H. A. Scrivener in the nineteenth century. By the time I was a student, I was introduced to the topic of method as a debate between these

---

11. Kilpatrick, "Western Text," 36. On the question of text-types in current discussion, see Gurry, "Text-Types."

12. Kilpatrick, "Western Text," 36.

13. Metzger, *Transmission, Corruption, and Restoration*, 175–79. Sturz does the same in *Byzantine Text-Type*, 16.

14. Metzger and Ehrman, *Transmission, Corruption, and Restoration*, 222–223. The change was introduced first in the fourth edition.

15. See the same point in Epp, "Eclectic Method," 142, a debate

three players.[16] Given how helpful I found that way of learning about method as a student, I have used it before myself,[17] and will do so here again—even though I am better aware now than I was before of what unites the two forms of eclecticism against the Byzantine priority position.

COMPETING APPROACHES

Byzantine Priority

The Byzantine priority position is named for its preference for a text found in the later and more numerous manuscripts copied during the Byzantine period. It appeals to its adherents because of its numerical advantage but also because it is close—though not exact—to the text behind the venerable (and venerated) King James Version. Those who accept it can take security in knowing that their text is found in most Greek manuscripts and in the most used English translation of all time.[18] The best version of this method was developed by Maurice Robinson and the late William Pierpont and has been developed and deployed most ably by them as well.[19]

Whatever the reasons for its appeal, it must be said clearly that the foundation of the approach is a *historical* claim about the text.[20] That claim is that a normal transmission process means the original text will most likely be found in a preponderance of witnesses. Why? Because a later majority is said to reflect an earlier

16. A major reason for that was the helpful placement of these three methods side-by-side in Black, *Rethinking*.

17. In my teaching, but also in Gurry, "Textual Criticism."

18. In my experience, pastors sometimes find in Byzantine priority a safe haven from the implausible arguments for the *textus receptus* on the one hand and the degree of human judgment required in eclecticism on the other.

19. Other versions of a majority text approach have been developed by Wilbur N. Pickering and Zane Hodges and Arthur Farstad.

20. The underlying view of the text's history is the key to explaining all three methods, a point I first learned from Michael Holmes (see, e.g., his chapter in *Rethinking*).

majority and scribes, overall, copied their texts faithfully.[21] Since the medieval Byzantine manuscripts far outnumber all others, this view leads us to the conclusion that the Byzantine text existed *prior to* the other texts like the Alexandrian and Western. If the Byzantine text has this historical priority, then it should also be given text-critical priority at any given point of variation. Practically, this means that, wherever there is a unity in the Byzantine witnesses, we can be confident we have the original text.[22] Where there is no such unity (or "preponderance"), decisions are made using all the same tools of internal evidence used in eclecticism. We might even say that, in such cases, the Byzantine prioritist becomes a kind of eclectic but who stays within the confines of the Byzantine manuscripts.

It's this last qualification, however, that most distinguishes Byzantine priority from eclecticism since it shows a consistent preference for *one* group of manuscripts to the exclusion of all others. There is never a place, for instance, where the Byzantine prioritist believes that the unified majority of manuscripts is flat wrong and the minority is right. Even if the Byzantine witnesses split, the choice will always be *within* that split and never from without. As an example, consider 1 John 2:23 which we can illustrate well enough from the NA[28] apparatus. Our critical texts read:

> πᾶς ὁ ἀρνούμενος τὸν υἱὸν οὐδὲ τὸν πατέρα ἔχει, ὁ ὁμολο-
> γῶν τὸν υἱὸν καὶ τὸν πατέρα ἔχει.

> Everyone who denies the Son neither has the Father; **the one who confesses the Son also has the Father.**

The Byzantine witnesses lack the entire second clause in bold and the reason is obvious enough to even the beginning student. It is a textbook case of *homoioteleuton*. The scribe's eye has simply skipped from the first τὸν πατέρα ἔχει ("has the Father") to the second so that the longer text is "unquestionably genuine," in the

---

21. Robinson in "Byzantine Priority," 11–23.

22. For the Robinson-Pierpont edition, this unity is determined using the apparatus of Hermann von Soden who, it should be said, was born in the greatest city in the world.

words of Scrivener.[23] But, because the Byzantine text is unified here in support of the shorter reading, the Byzantine prioritist is committed to the shorter reading and must reject the obvious explanation (along with many early witnesses). As I see it, this variant is a near-perfect test case for the Byzantine priority approach—one that it fails. And this is not a lone example (see, e.g., 1 Cor 9:20; Jas 4:12; 1 John 3:1; Jude 25 where the Byzantine text has the shorter reading due to *homoioteleuton*).

Because of this, the Byzantine priority position, unlike the approach of Scrivener, becomes, in practice, a Byzantine exclusivism. It is a position which never thinks its preferred manuscripts are altogether wrong. This is what most distinguishes the position. It is *not* first and foremost its preference for the Byzantine witnesses per se, but its belief that the original text is *always* found within one set of manuscripts. Such exclusivity is its distinguishing feature. It is on that question that it disagrees most with all other methods, and on that point that I have my strongest objections.[24]

Thoroughgoing Eclecticism

Quite different is the approach of thoroughgoing eclecticism, which we encountered with Kilpatrick. Today, its most able practitioner and theorist is J. K. Elliott with further examples in the work of Jeffrey Kloha on 1 Corinthians and Charles Landon on Jude.[25] Thoroughgoing eclecticism holds that present-day knowledge of manuscript relations is too uncertain to allow us to think that any single manuscript, however old, or any set of manuscripts, however numerous, should be given the benefit of the doubt. As Landon says, "thoroughgoing ecleciticism is unfettered from adherence to the range of external canons which channels our preferences in

23. Scrivener, *Plain Introduction*, 400.

24. It is what I have called the "all or nothing" problem. See Gurry, "All-or-Nothing Problem." Even at their most partisan, Tischendorf did not think Sinaiticus was *always* right nor Westcott and Hort, Vaticanus.

25. See Elliott, *New Testament Textual Criticism*, 137; Kloha, "Textual Commentary"; Landon, *Jude*, 135.

the narrow direction of a 'best' MS or a 'best' group of MSS."[26] As a result, thoroughgoing eclectics view manuscript preferences with suspicion and sometimes speak pejoratively about the "cult of the best manuscripts."[27] In this, it works as a kind of mirror image to the Byzantine priority position. Variants are approached primarily on stylistic and grammatical grounds with careful consideration for the changes in Greek language and the tendencies of scribes to change their texts. There is little or no concern for claims about the best manuscripts or groups of manuscripts. What counts far more than the age or text-type of a manuscript is whether a reading fits with an author's known style of writing or with what is thought to be Greek typical of the time. In this, it fronts internal evidence instead of external. The result can be readings that are accepted with very slim external support; the danger is that the critic's own judgments about an author's style become tyrannical. Finally, there is the problem of a kind of willful ignorance. After all, once the thoroughgoing eclectic has determined the most likely original text in enough places, that data should be used to evaluate the relative quality of the manuscripts. That knowledge would, in turn, be useful for solving remaining problems. In Landon's case, for example, he offers a statistical evaluation of manuscripts based on how often they have the correct reading (as determined by internal criteria) and how often they didn't. The results show Vaticanus to be right in 74 percent of cases whereas 044 is right in 54 percent.[28] How can the thoroughgoing eclectic see these results and still claim that there is no such thing as a "best manuscript"? By his own judgment, there is. My basic objection to thoroughgoing eclecticism, then, is that it does not take enough account of its own results.[29]

26. Landon, *Jude*, 16.

27. Elliott, "Thoroughgoing Eclecticism," 101–24.

28. Landon, *Jude*, 148. Vaticanus is correct in 70 of 95 cases and 044 (Ψ) in 51.

29. For more on this point, see Gurry, *Critical Examination*, 102–105, 107.

Reasoned Eclecticism

The dominant view among New Testament scholars is reasoned eclecticism and has been used to edit the most recent editions of the Greek New Testament (SBLGNT, NA[28]/UBS[5], THGNT). Unlike the Byzantine priority position, this view holds that the New Testament text has suffered from significant contamination and is thus not "normal." But, unlike the approach of thoroughgoing eclecticism, it also holds that this contamination is not so severe that we cannot say anything positive about manuscript relations or their relative value.[30] It is considered "reasoned" because judgments are based on both internal and external evidence. The name is a bit self-serving in my view, but it is now standard parlance and I am in no position to change it. The salient feature is that neither internal nor external evidence ever makes a consideration of the other unnecessary in the effort to identify the original text. A set of well-worn criteria can be summed up in the principle that the reading that best accounts for how the other(s) developed should be preferred. As an "eclectic" method, this principle must be applied on a case-by-case basis, sometimes following one witness, sometimes another. As E. C. Colwell put it in 1952:

> We cannot choose our New Testament by counting noses, or by venerating age, or by the selection of a paragon, or by constructing a family tree, or by preferring an early Christian who commented on the New Testament to one who copied it, or by assuming the independence of witnesses from distant places.[31]

Instead, the best New Testament is the one chosen verse by verse by comparing both external and internal evidence. Or, in the more recent words of Tommy Wasserman, "Since no single manuscript, manuscript family, or larger group of manuscripts (a *text type*) can be accepted uncritically as representing the original version

---

30. Fee, "Rigorous or Reasoned," 127. I am in large agreement with his general critique.

31. Colwell, *Best New Testament*, 72.

of a biblical passage or book, the various extant witnesses must be evaluated passage by passage."[32]

It is important to point out that reasoned eclecticism, as explained here, does not say whether internal or external criteria is more important. Nor does it prescribe which one should be appealed to first and foremost.[33] Nor does it say which manuscripts or groups of manuscripts are best. This is intentional as I have tried to present the basic principle broadly enough to encompass a variety of practitioners. The essential feature of the approach, as I conceive it, is that it neither appeals to one group exclusively nor rejects all groups equally. Any approach that does this falls under the banner of reasoned eclecticism. Speaking for myself, I am skeptical of attempts to define text-types and then relate them genealogically[34] and I may be a bit more willing to depart from the earliest witnesses than some of my fellow reasoned eclectics. No matter. We are still operating from the same basic principle; we just disagree on the details.

AN ADVANTAGE, EXAMPLE, AND OBJECTION

This is a basic explanation of the method in contrast to the others on offer. But more can be said in its favor by offering some comments on its main advantage, providing an illustration of it, and then responding to a common objection to it. First, the advantage.

32. Wasserman, "Textual Criticism," 407–17 (414); emphasis original.

33. For myself, I think internal evidence should be used in as many clear cases as possible to make an initial judgment about the relative value of the witnesses. The relative quality of the witnesses can then be used to further support (or challenge) our decisions. Where internal criteria conflict, we should follow the witnesses that have proven themselves reliable most often in the clear cases. So, I might reverse Vaganay's colorful expression and say that *external* evidence is a servant, but when the master is away, the subordinates must be at the ready to bear responsibility (*Introduction*, 93).

34. This is why I cannot accept the version of reasoned eclecticism espoused by Sturz in *Byzantine Text-Type*. Though he rightly shows that the later Byzantine text has early roots, I cannot accept his conclusion that the major text-types are independent of one another. Text-types are simply not defined well enough for that (see Gurry, "Text-Types").

Advantage

One of the main advantages I see of reasoned eclecticism is that it is based on what we know not on what we don't. Byzantine priority depends on the absence of evidence in the case of early Byzantine witnesses (I speak of *witnesses* not readings). But even if we had them, that would only point us in the direction of a Sturzian approach not a Byzantine priority one.[35] I see no basis for thinking that the unified Byzantine text is always right just as I don't think it's always wrong. There are times, where the internal evidence is so strong, that I am happy to follow the Byzantine reading even when it goes against the earliest witnesses.[36] But there are also places, such as 1 John 2:23 where the same internal evidence shows that the Byzantine text cannot be right.

In the case of thoroughgoing eclecticism, it depends on a lack of knowledge about manuscript relationships which I find untenable. We may not know all we want to know about the history of the text, and we may not agree on exactly how to use what we do know, but we know too much that can't be denied to become agnostic about the number, date, or quality of witnesses at our disposal. If some have been prone to a "cult" of the best manuscripts, the remedy is not found in flattening all manuscripts as equals. One overreaction is not fixed by another. In this regard, Fee was right to say that, if Hort's "evaluation of B as 'neutral' was too high a regard for that MS, it does not alter his judgment that compared to all other MSS B *is* a superior witness."[37]

In sum, we know enough about the history of the text to know that (1) some manuscripts are better than others; that (2) no single manuscript is always right; and that (3) no single group of manuscripts, even when unified, is never wrong. The result is the need to weigh both internal and external criteria with a mind well informed by the manuscripts themselves and the mistakes made by the scribes who copied them.

35. See Sturz, *Byzantine Text-Type*, 130.

36. For some examples, see Gurry, "Shorter Reading," 122–41.

37. Fee, "Rigorous or Reasoned," 127.

Mark 1:2

An example will help illustrate the method. Mark's Gospel introduces John the Baptist's ministry with a blended citation of Mal 3:1 (and Exod 23:20?) with Isa 40:3. Mark introduces this as being written prophetically. That much is clear. What is not clear is whether he identifies the source as Isaiah in particular or the prophets in general. In the new *Editio Critica Maior* (ECM), there are five readings attested, the first two of which I combine here for ease since only the article is in question.[38]

1. ἐν (τῷ) Ἡσαΐᾳ τῷ προφήτῃ (in Isaiah the prophet)
   01. 03. 05. 019r. 037. 038. 1. 33. 61. 131. 152. 176r. 184. 205. 209. 222. 348. 372. 555. 565. 700r. 728. 829. 872*V. 873. 892. 1071r. 1241. 1243. 1279. 1579. 1582r. 2174. 2193*. 2486. 2737. 2886. L844. L2211. AnastS. Bas. Epiph. HesH. Ir. Or. PsAth. Serap. SevGab. TitB. OrLat. L:DIV. K:SB⸃. S:PH^M. CPA:CL. Go

2. ἐν βίβλῳ λόγων Ἡσαΐου τοῦ προφήτου (in the book of the words of Isaiah the prophet; cf. Luke 3:4)
   544. 1273. 2680r

3. ἐν προφήτῃ (in a prophet)
   872C

4. ἐν τοῖς προφήταις (in the prophets)
   02. 032. 13. 28. 69. 124. 346. 427. 543. 579. 732. 788. 792r. 826. 828. 837. 983. 1342. 1424. 1689. 2193A. 2542. L547. Byz [791r. L6or. L387r]. AstS. GermC. IrLat. Phot. L:I^alt. S:H^T. Ä

Two of these readings are easily rejected by any method. The second has the marks of a harmonization to Luke 3:4 which also quotes Isa 40:3. The third reading, in 872, is a correction that appears to be an erasure designed to turn Ἡσαΐᾳ τῷ προφήτῃ into

---

38. This also allows me to combine the patristic and versional witnesses whose support for the article before Ἡσαΐᾳ is inconclusive (marked "a/b" in the ECM apparatus).

ἐν προφήταις. This is actually an important clue as to which text scribes in the Middle Ages felt was more appropriate. Since the citation is not just from Isa 40:3, they seemed to have felt discomfort attributing it only to Isaiah. Just as the later scribe of 872 did, so an early scribe probably smoothed the issue out by a simple change.[39] Such "correcting" of a manuscript was hardly unusual in a world where no two copies of an ancient work were the same and mistakes were expected.[40] On the other hand, where the other Gospels quote Isa 40:3 (Matt 3:3; Luke 3:4; John 1:19–23), they all identify Isaiah as the source and so a scribe may have been influenced to *add* his name here to harmonize. On any account, harmonization certainly accounts for reading two so it can be ruled out. Another explanation is that scribes wanted to fill the "void" of the generic "prophets" with Isaiah. But why name only Isaiah in that case? In terms of Mark's style and theology, it's easy enough to see why he would highlight Isaiah given his influence on Mark's theology.[41] Isaiah will be mentioned again by name in Mark 7:6. All these are internal considerations and here the reasoned eclectic must turn to external as well. There we find strong support for "Isaiah" in the earliest and, yes, best Greek manuscripts (01, 03, 05) as well as in early Fathers (Origen, Irenaeus, Epiphanius) and early versions (Old Latin, Syriac Peshitta, Coptic). In other words, where the internal evidence points slightly in favor of "in Isaiah," the external evidence clearly does.

Objection

If this is how the method works in practice, it remains to answer an important objection that says any form of eclecticism is flawed because it will inevitably produce a Frankenstein text. Such a text was never actually used by Christians until we created it in the lab

---

39. Though ECM lists 872C as supporting προφήτῃ, the -ῃ has been erased, I take it, so it can be read as a plural.

40. For the expectation of emendation in punctuation at least, see Parkes, *Pause and Effect*, 12.

41. See, Watts, *Isaiah's New Exodus*; Moyise, "Composite Citations," 17–25.

and shocked it into life. It's based on the idiosyncrasies of modern scholars, it can never lead to an agreement about the original text, and, as such, it lacks historical and even theological authority.

This argument is sometimes expressed inelegantly (but highly entertainingly) in online cartoons.[42] But let us focus on the more serious and detailed form of the argument made by Maurice Robinson. In a 2009 essay, Robinson identified over one hundred verses in the standard critical edition (the NA[27] at the time) that did not exist in their entirety in any known manuscript, version, or church father. The use of eclecticism, in other words, resulted in a text in these places with zero support and thereby uncovered "an inherent problem within the various forms of eclectic methodology."[43] A later, unpublished study revealed two hundred and ten more places where two verse segments had the same zero support. The problem this presents us with is that "the resultant text—even within relatively short segments—becomes an entity that apparently never existed at any time or place." And ultimately, that leaves us with "questionable results regarding theological textual confidence as a by-product."[44] Do we want to stake our faith on a Frankenstein text? The answer from these critics is no. The solution offered is found in the Byzantine text, or the Majority Text, or perhaps the *textus receptus*, depending on who is raising the objection.

But the basis for the criticism is unsound. The first indication of this is that it conflicts with another frequent criticism of the eclectic text, namely, that it is too hidebound to Codex Sinaiticus and Codex Vaticanus. This has been the charge since at least Burgon's day and remains a favorite of King James Onlysists. But which is it? Is the eclectic text wrong because it's too similar to Sinaiticus and Vaticanus or is it wrong because its text never existed at any time or place? These arguments are running in opposite directions. They can't both be right. They can, however, both be wrong.

42. See Sheffield, "Textual Frankenstein."
43. Robinson, "Rule 9," 34.
44. His own summary in Robinson, "Autograph Originality."

To illustrate the problem, let us consider the most ambitious eclectic edition made in over one hundred years, the still-in-progress *Editio Critica Maior*. These volumes, now available for Mark, Acts, and the Catholic Letters, have huge amounts of data collected from over one hundred manuscripts per book. Best of all, the digital data behind them can be compared statistically with just a few clicks at https://ntvmr.uni-muenster.de/. When we do so, we find that the editors' text, produced using reasoned eclecticism, agrees with Codex Vaticanus at over 96 percent of the fifteen thousand or so places of variation. Their agreement with Sinaiticus is over 90 percent. These two manuscripts are both early and substantial, containing all or most of the New Testament.[45] But there are also much later manuscripts that show similar levels of agreement such as minuscule 81 that dates to 1044 AD, some six hundred years later. These levels of agreement, spread across so many places of variation, do not suggest to me a Frankenstein text.

That provides what I think is an initial response, but we can go further still. The real problem with Robinson's objection is methodological. He has not used the right tool for the job. If one wants to see where the eclectic text is unsupported in verse segments, we need a better apparatus than the one in a small hand edition like the NA[27]. To see if this is the case, I spot-checked Robinson's examples where we have ECM data. I give three examples.

In Mark 11:3, the ECM does show that the NA[27] verse is not represented in full because of a singular reading in 03. The ECM has changed its text in one of the variants in NA[27] by printing ὅτι as the initial text (the other variant now has a diamond). The result is that the verse as a whole finds support in 01, 019, 579, 892, 2766. In Acts 2:7, the entire verse as printed in NA[27] has the support of P74 once we ignore the spelling difference between οὐκ and οὐχ and excepting the two first words that aren't in P74 because it is fragmentary. Minuscule 383 also agrees fully with NA[27] except in two letters, having οὐκ and παντες for ἄπαντες. The latter is a

---

45. To the reader who claims victory at these stats ("See! They are slaves to Sinaiticus and Vaticanus"), I gladly concede that I prefer a critical text that aligns closely with the text of our best manuscripts. That's as it should be.

choice between two words whose distinction the standard NT Greek dictionary says "is not maintained in the NT."[46] In the case of Acts 27:8, the ECM has again changed slightly from NA^{27} and so it has the support of 01, 33, 206C, 429, 522f, 1490, 1831.

Now, I suspect that, in all of Robinson's examples, he may still find verses with "zero support" even in the ECM. But what does this tell us, really? It may tell us that reasoned eclectics sometimes don't pay enough attention to the surrounding variant units when they make their decisions. This is a fault I have caught myself making and I think eclectics do need to be careful about it. I am optimistic that the CBGM is one way to help with that and, as a small token, the fact that two of Robinson's examples have been "fixed" by the ECM shows promise. But secondly, I think whatever Robinson's examples remain after using a better apparatus tell us what we already know: the NT is a highly contaminated textual tradition—perhaps the most contaminated we know of. In such a tradition, it will certainly be the case that in certain segments of the reconstructed text, there will be no single manuscript that attests to the entire segment. That is what contamination does and so that is what an edition of the original text should look like.

In summary, I do not think that Robinson's examples do anything except remind us why we need an eclectic method in the first place. That our resulting text is, in fact, eclectic is exactly what we should expect. What it is not, is so wildly eclectic that we should fear it being unleashed on the public like Dr. Frankenstein's monster. Instead, it provides what a scholarly edition of a contaminated textual tradition should look like.

CONCLUSION

I have tried to explain what the most widely used method is for identifying the original text of the New Testament amongst our thousands of manuscripts, all of which have suffered, to varying degrees from scribal mistakes. That method is known as reasoned

---

46. BDAG, s.v. ἅπας (p. 98).

eclecticism. I compared it to competing approaches and explained why I think it is better. I explained the advantages, illustrated the method from Mark 1:2, and tried to answer what I consider to be the most important objection to the method from its critics.

To summarize, then, the basic feature of reasoned eclecticism is that both internal and external evidence must be used in combination, neither one being neglected. Because of contamination, each place of variation must be approached with fresh eyes, informed but not enslaved by the editor's previous decisions. Manuscripts should be weighed and evaluated so that their differences can be recognized and appreciated. At the same time, no one manuscript (or group) can be treated as miraculously preserving the original text. In all this, the reasoned eclectic must be worthy of the adjective by keeping his wits about him. There is no substitute for *thinking*. Such thinking reminds us that we have made it this far without quoting A. E. Housman, but there is no point in resisting further:

> A textual critic engaged upon his business is not at all like Newton investigating the motions of the planets: he is much more like a dog hunting for fleas. If a dog hunted for fleas on mathematical principles, basing his researches on statistics of area and population, he would never catch a flea except by accident. They require to be treated as individuals; and every problem which presents itself to the textual critic must be regarded as possibly unique.[47]

That is a description of reasoned eclecticism. It is a method that recognizes we are dealing with the vagaries of human copying and so nothing less will do than the careful application of human judgment at each place where decision must be made. We do this, not by appeal to whimsy or private prejudice nor based on what we would have liked the New Testament writers to have said, but informed by all the knowledge we can muster about scribes, their handiwork, and the authors whose words they preserved for us over so many centuries.[48]

47. Housman, "Application."

48. My thanks to my fellow speakers, the attendees, and to Elijah Hixson for helpful feedback on earlier versions of this chapter.

Chapter 3

A BYZANTINE-PRIORITY PERSPECTIVE REGARDING THE RECOGNITION OF AUTOGRAPH ORIGINALITY

MAURICE A. ROBINSON

The Christian biblical scholar has as his God-given task the study of scripture. He does it not as a mere secular job but in the consciousness that he is handling the Word of God and that what he is doing is of immense practical and spiritual importance for the church.

—James Barr[1]

CERTAINLY, THE TEXT OF the New Testament as it appears among the various MSS, textual clusters, versions, and translations, is clearly an adequate representation of the inspired autographs. Appeal can be made at any time to most individual MSS or to their aggregate consensus readings as authoritative, mainly because they

---

1. Barr, *Canon, Authority, Criticism*, 110.

approximate each other closely and remain substantially identical to the originals.

That the inspired text of the New Testament books should be presented in an accurate and precise form that represents its original first-century composition is not a mere philosophical abstraction, but serves as a primary reason for accepting the sacred text as authoritative for doctrinal, ethical and moral purposes.[2] As Scrivener noted in 1853:

> The criticism of the text of Holy Scripture, though confessedly inferior in point of dignity and importance to its right interpretation, yet takes precedence of it in order of time: for how can we consistently proceed to investigate the sense of the Sacred Volume, till we have done our utmost to ascertain its precise words?[3]

Textual criticism necessarily arises, not from a desire to alter or corrupt the biblical text, but because of the need to establish the text on a firm basis in view of the various readings that exist among the five thousand-plus manuscripts (MSS) that have been transmitted throughout copying history. Obviously, where variation occurs, only *one* reading can possibly reflect the autograph while potential alternatives would fail to do so. The problem is how to resolve such instances of variant readings appearing among the MSS in a manner that not only honors but preserves the intent of the original human writers. This is where the discipline of textual criticism comes into application, and if all textual critics agreed in regard to a single reading in every unit of textual variation, then the task of establishing the autograph form of every New Testament (NT) book already would be complete, with nothing more required.

---

2. As Paul states: "All Scripture is breathed out by God and profitable for teaching, for reproof, for correction, and for training in righteousness, that the man of God may be complete, equipped for every good work"; also 1 Pet 1:21, "Holy men of God spoke as they were carried along by the Holy Spirit" (ESV, adjusted to reflect the Byzantine Textform).

3. Scrivener, *Twenty Greek Manuscripts*, ix.

However, as with all humanly based endeavors, differing theories and methodologies have been offered, each claiming an optimal way to establish the NT autographic text based upon particular principles (many good, but others questionable). The primary methods encountered at present are known as reasoned eclecticism, thoroughgoing eclecticism, and Byzantine priority (sometimes termed the "majority text" position). Obviously, where all three schools of textual scholarship agree, the conclusions reached offer a strong presumption regarding autograph originality at such points—and this in fact encompasses the overwhelming bulk of the entire NT text, which by a collation-based comparison of the differing extremes between the NA[27] base text and the Byzantine Textform results in an overall level of textual "authenticity agreement" of approximately 94 percent,[4] with individual narrative segments (termed "pericopes") often displaying an even higher amount of agreement. To cite an extended sample pericope to illustrate this principle:

The Prodigal Son

The twenty-two-verse parable of the Prodigal Son (Luke 15:11–32) encompasses three hundred and ninety-five words in the Byzantine Textform and three hundred and seventy-three words in the NA[27] critical edition.[5] The two texts agree *precisely* regarding three hundred and sixty-five words—a percentage of agreement of 92.4% relative to the Byzantine text, and 97.8% relative to the NA[27] text—resulting in an average support percentage of 95.1%. Also within this twenty-two-verse passage, NA[27] and the Byzantine Textform have *no* variation whatever in the following six verses: Luke 15: 11, 15, 18, 25, 27, 31.

4. The collated differences appear as footnotes in Robinson and Pierpont, *Byzantine Textform*.

5. Word-count statistics (excluding verse numbers) tabulated both by Microsoft Word and the Wordstat software program developed by Robert Rinker of Jacksonville, Florida.

More important than mere statistics, however, is the *nature* of the variants observed in this parable; namely, how many of the variants are substantial (i.e., translationally meaningful or with some degree of exegetical significance) and how many merely involve orthographic or word order alteration. An examination of the variants within the passage will demonstrate the paucity of issues involved in those instances where the NA[27] critical text differs from the Byzantine Textform (readings marked with an asterisk are *not* noted in the NA[27] apparatus);[6] actual translational differences are noted by bold underline and an arrow (→):

Lk 15:	NA	Byzantine (𝔐)	Translation
12	ο δε	και	**But** → **and**
13	παντα	απαντα	all
14	ισχυρα	ισχυρος	mighty
16	χορτασθηναι	γεμισαι την χοιλιαν αυτου	**be satisfied** → **fill his belly**
16	εχ	απο	**out of** → **from**
*17	εφη	ειπεν	he **was saying** → he **said**
17	περισσευονται	περισσευουσιν	they abound
17	λιμω ωδε	λιμω	famine **here** → famine
*19	ουχετι	χαι ουχετι	no longer → **and** no longer
20	εαυτου (𝔐ₚₜ)	αυτου (𝔐ₚₜ)	his
21	ειπεν δε ο υιος αυτω	ειπεν δε αυτω ο υιος	but the son said to him
*21	ουχετι	χαι ουχετι	no longer → **and** no longer
22	ταχυ	—	quickly
22	στολην την στολην	την στολην	**a** robe → **the** robe

6. Regarding Byzantine readings *not* cited in the NA[27] apparatus, see Robinson, "All About Variants," 116–53.

23	φερετε	ενεγκαντες	**bring** → **having brought**
24	ην απολωλως	και απολωλως	had perished
26	τί αν ειη ταυτα	τί ειη ταυτα	what might these be
*28	δε	ουν	**but** → **therefore**
29	πατρι αυτου	πατρι	**his** father → **the** father
30	τον σιτευτον μοσχον	τον μοσχον τον σιτευτον	the fattened calf
32	εζησεν	ανεζησεν	lives → lives **again**
32	και απολωλως	και απολωλως ην	and perished → and **was** perished

An Early Papyrus Page

A more direct example, returning similar results, comes from comparing a single page (John 3:14–20) from one of the earliest papyri reflecting the Alexandrian type of text underlying the modern critical editions (p75, closely aligned with Vaticanus B/03), and comparing its precise wording against the supposedly "later" Byzantine Textform. The collation result for this one hundred and thirty-six-word segment comprising five hundred and sixty-one letters written in uncial script is as follows (English translatable variants noted again by bold underline):

Collation	**English as affected**
14 Μωσης) [Μω]υσης (begin page)	*Spelling variation for* "Moses"
15 εις) εν αυτω	**into** him) **in** him
μη αποληται αλλ) —	**_Omit_** **"should not perish but"**
16 τον υιον αυτου) τον υιον	**his** Son) **the** Son
17 τον υιον αυτου) τον υιον	**his** Son) **the** Son
19 οι ανθρωποι μαλλον) μαλλον οι ανθρωποι	*Word order:* "the men rather" versus "rather the men" (both with same meaning).

πονηρα αυτων) αυτων πονηρα	*Word order:* "evil of them" vs "of them evil" (both meaning "their evil)
20 [ερχεται]	*Last word on page*

This sample, taken from an extremely early manuscript, shows only twelve words out of one hundred and thirty-six (8.8%) to differ; of these, only six out of one hundred and thirty-six (4.4%) actually affect translation—and that minimally.[7] This serves to illustrate how minor most variants happen to be, whether considered from the perspective of the critical text or the Byzantine Textform. As Robert Renehan stated in regard to secular Greek classical literature, "The MSS far more frequently than not preserve *exactly* what the author wrote."[8] This is further illustrated by the Alands' observation that, "apart from orthographical differences," out of the seven thousand, nine hundred and forty-seven total verses in the Greek NT, four thousand, nine hundred and ninety-nine of them (62.9 percent) have *no* cited variants in any of the seven major critical editions (Tischendorf, Westcott-Hort, von Soden, Vogels, Merk, Bover, NA^{25}).[9]

Data such as these relate to what constitutes a level of "Byzantine support" when viewed from a Byzantine priority position. The distinctions are interesting:

1. ***All***—In regard to the *ca.* 94 percent of the text where the critical text and Byzantine Textform concur, virtually *everyone* actually supports the Byzantine or "majority text."

2. ***Some***—In the remaining *ca.* 6 percent of the text where variation occurs (including even minor orthographic variation), while pro-Byzantine advocates simply follow that texttype, most critical scholars (generally pro-Alexandrian) continue to support *some* Byzantine readings even while maintaining

---

7. Note that the p75 transposition ~ μαλλον οι ανθρωποι at Jn 3:17 differs from *both* Byz and NA^{27}, which read in common οι ανθρωποι μαλλον.

8. Renehan, *Greek Textual Criticism*, 2 (emphasis added).

9. Aland and Aland, *Introduction*, 28–29. A table also shows a book-by-book breakdown regarding variant-free verses.

their overall *non*-Byzantine position. For example, in the Prodigal Son at Luke 15:19, virtually all critics reject the second inclusion of the phrase ποιησον με ως ενα των μισθιων σου ("make me as one of your hired servants"), despite the extremely strong support from א. B. D. 33. 700. 1241. l844—a phrase that normally should be considered to reflect an "Alexandrian archetype" reading. There also remain numerous Byzantine readings (cited as 𝕸) that also support the NA main text against various minority readings—a situation now further enhanced by the acceptance of dozens of previously rejected Byzantine readings as a result of the Coherence-Based Genealogical Method (CBGM) currently enjoying a particular degree of influence among critical scholarship.

3. ***None***—This leaves among the *ca.* 6 percent a small percentage of variant readings where critical scholars continue to follow the nineteenth-century editorial judgments that had rejected any concept of Byzantine originality (e.g. Lachmann, Tischendorf, Tregelles, Westcott-Hort).

4. ***Who knows?*** This category encompasses the relatively large number of variant units where all MSS are sufficiently divided so as to present some difficulty of resolution (even for pro-Byzantine advocates). Many of these are indicated in the NA critical apparatus as having "*pm*" (*permulti*) support for more than one possible reading, while some of these are noted as marginal alternatives within the Byzantine Textform edition.

Despite these observations, there remains a significant divide regarding text-critical presuppositions, theory, and methodology, generally characterized under the particular forms of eclecticism (reasoned, thoroughgoing) favoring a basically Alexandrian type of text, or those in varying degrees supportive of *some* form of the Byzantine Textform (Byzantine priority, "majority text," the methodology of Harry Sturz, the "Equitable eclecticism" approach of James Snapp, or even the so-called Confessional Bibliology position that basically favors a form of the printed TR). Obviously, presuppositional, theoretical, and methodological differences exist among these varying positions, the resultant readings favored by each changing the text within the *ca.* 6 percent of the NT where significant variation occurs. In general, the several eclectic approaches strongly favor a primarily Alexandrian type of cluster, while the other, more traditional textual supporters tend to favor a mostly Byzantine-type cluster, even while otherwise agreed regarding the remaining *ca.* 94 percent of the New Testament text.

Given the underlying presuppositions that shape these theories and affect their strategies for approaching the text, the varying presuppositions, theories, and methodologies of the respective text-critical positions should be considered from the standpoint of a "hermeneutics of suspicion" that "questions traditional interpretations . . . . about the origin of a text, as well as about the biases of modern interpreters."[10] With certain adjustments, even a political writer like George Will can make an important observation regarding text-critical matters:

> A person's text-critical judgments are not random . . . .
> What might be commonly thought to represent a certain position at any given point should be carefully pried apart and examined . . . . One should aim to recast textual criticism in a form compatible with what would normally be expected in the transmissional history of MSS that held a specific religious value to those who copied and promulgated them.[11]

Significantly, the nineteenth-century approach to New Testament Textual Criticism (NTTC) was characterized by a primary appeal to external testimony (meaning the testimony of MSS, ancient versions, and early church writers) rather than focusing on various internal criteria involving *transcriptional probability* (the alterations or errors scribes were inclined to make) and *intrinsic*

10. The phrases (in a quite different context!) are from Strouse, "Magnificat!" (Strouse declares herself to be "a 'proud member of the religious left' and an unapologetic progressive Christian").

11. See Will, *Statecraft*, 11–12. Will's original comment has been modified, paraphrased, restated, and reapplied to NT textual criticism by the present writer.

probability (what a given NT author would most likely have written based on considerations of vocabulary, style, syntax, themes, and emphases).[12] In this regard, with external evidence as primary, scholars such as Lachmann, Tischendorf, Tregelles, and Westcott-Hort followed the most reasonable path. A common weakness influencing their external approach, however, was their (at the time quite reasonable) preference for the earliest available manuscripts, coupled with a systematic and somewhat hostile rejection of the general consensus text found in the mass of (mostly later) Byzantine MSS, [13] as primarily (but not entirely) reflected in the available but questionably supported printed TR editions.[14] Had such animosity not been a leading factor, their respective texts might have looked much different than the prevailing Alexandrian type of text currently reflected among our critical editions. This is not to say that a primarily external approach was erroneous: only that certain aspects involving presuppositions and methodology unavoidably biased their results.[15]

12. The terms are those of Westcott and Hort, "Introduction," 20–22 (Intrinsic probability), and 22–30 (transcriptional probability).

13. As noted by Fee, "Rigorous and Reasoned," 177: "Whether justified or not, Hort used genealogy *solely* to dispense with the Syrian (Byzantine) text" (emphasis added).

14. Cf. Hort's sentiment expressed in 1851 at age twenty-three: "I had no idea till the last few weeks of the importance of texts, having read so little Greek Testament, and dragged on with the villainous *Textus Receptus* . . . . Bagster's *Critical,* which has Scholz's text, . . . with parallel Greek and English . . . . pleased me much; so many little alterations on good MS. authority made things clear not in a vulgar, notional way, but by giving a deeper and fuller meaning . . . . Tischendorf I find a great acquisition, above all, because he gives the various readings at the bottom of his page, and his Prolegomena are invaluable. Think of that vile *Textus Receptus* leaning entirely on late MSS.; it is a blessing there are such early ones." (*Letter to the Rev. John Ellerton,* 29–30, in Hort, *Life and Letters,* 1:211).

15. Cosaert, *Clement of Alexandria,* 306, notes that "Westcott and Hort's total disregard of all Byzantine readings as secondary is too severe"—this even though Cosaert himself considers the Byzantine Textform late and secondary, having "originated not as a creation but as a process of choosing between early readings" (231n31).

On the other hand, one cannot simply presume a theory and its accompanying methodology to be erroneous, biased, or distorted merely because certain practitioners accept and advocate its validity. Presuppositions and contrasts with prior theories and attempted methods need to be considered, along with whatever changes and refinements might have led to a given hypothesis. It is one matter narrowly to follow and accept what one has been taught without question or investigation; it is quite another undertaking for someone to begin from a particular position and to transition from that into a different conclusion following extensive critical research and investigation that concludes the prior hypothesis to be defective in some manner rectified by the alternate theory. For example, the Byzantine priority hypothesis recognizes that Westcott and Hort (who remain the primary influencers of modern textual criticism) were correct on several major points:

- Textual criticism without a history of the text is impossible;

- MSS should be grouped according to their textual clusters and families;

- The origin of such textual clusters needs to be accounted for;

- Individual documents need careful examination, particularly in relation to the habits and proclivities of their respective scribes;

- The establishment of the original text is primarily a matter of external evidence.

- Internal criteria must be applied with care, being essentially subjective by nature and often selectively applied;

- Assuming a normal process of textual transmission (i.e., without recensional intervention), "a majority of extant documents is more likely to reflect a majority of ancestral documents *at each stage of transmission* than *vice versa.*"[16]

In all of these points, Westcott and Hort were actually *more* correct than that of most modern eclectics, whether reasoned or

---

16. Westcott and Hort, "Introduction," 45 (emphasis added).

rigorous.[17] Although most modern eclectics might object), a judicious application of Westcott-Hort, based impartially on just those principles could easily result in a text more closely resembling a carefully nuanced form of Byzantine priority than anything provided by an eclectically determined critical edition.

CONTEMPORARY ECLECTICISM— ΕΣΤΑΘΗ ΕΝ ΖΥΓΩι ΚΑΙ ΕΥΡΕΘΗ ΥΣΤΕΡΟΥΣΑ.[18]

In contrast, contemporary eclectic textual criticism has moved away from the Westcott-Hort theory and method, although in practice the text formed by means of either reasoned or thoroughgoing eclecticism continues to reflect a resultant text mostly comparable to that established by Westcott and Hort,[19] in which even the current critical editions' "patchwork at numerous spots in the text of Westcott and Hort is no more than temporary repair."[20] As Kenneth W. Clark noted seven decades ago:

> It is very important to recognize that *it* [Eclecticism] *is a secondary and tentative method. It is not a new method nor a permanent one.* The eclectic method cannot by itself create a text to displace Westcott-Hort and its off-spring. *It is suitable only for exploration and experimentation.*[21]

17. This is not to say that Westcott and Hort were totally correct. Rather, they erred in several areas (e.g., their assertions regarding a "Syrian [= Byzantine] recension," genealogical stemmata, Byzantine conflation, smoothing and harmonizing, and "distinctive" Byzantine readings)—but these are not the primary focus of concern at this point.

18. Dan 5:27 LXX: "It has been placed in the balance scale and found lacking."

19. Cf. Clark, "Today's Problems," 159–60: "All the critical editions since 1881 are basically the same as Westcott-Hort. All are founded on the same Egyptian recension, and generally reflect the same assumptions of transmission . . . . Each of them is basically a repetition of the Westcott-Hort text . . . . We have continued . . . to live in the era of Westcott-Hort, our *textus receptus.*"

20. Clark, "Manuscripts," 19.

21. Clark, "Effect," 37–38, emphasis added.

And even Westcott and Hort in their own day offered harsh words regarding eclecticism:

> All decisions made solely or chiefly on the ground of internal evidence are subject to the chances of mistake inseparable from single and isolated judgements; they lack the security given by comparison and mutual correction. Hence *it is dangerous to fix the mind in the first instance on any kind of internal probability: the bias thus inevitably acquired can hardly fail to mislead* where the authority of documents is not obviously clear and decisive at once. The uses of internal evidence are subordinate and accessory: *if taken as the primary guide, it cannot but lead to extensive error.*[22]

In contrast to contemporary eclectic procedure, Kenneth W. Clark in a personal interview offered a most radical and somewhat surprising solution:

> We will finally have to find a texttype or a manuscript that can be followed to the bitter end as authoritative, or we are merely making educated guesses as to what the autographs might be. A constructed text will not do . . . . We are not finding the original text where we ought to find it, so let's look where we don't expect it.[23]

Modern eclecticism, however, continues to typify most practitioners of NTTC. Like the inevitable "temporary taxes" imposed by politicians, once entrenched the effect becomes not only permanent, but nearly impossible to dislodge (the current CBGM supposedly was intended to alleviate that problem, but even so, its overall resultant *Ausgangstext* still resembles that of Westcott and Hort more than anything else). As Robert M. Grant suggested, "We are left in the quagmire of disintegrative specialization."[24]

---

22. Westcott and Hort, *New Testament in the Original Greek*, 1:542–43 (emphasis added).

23. Kenneth W. Clark, personal interview with the present writer, 3 May 1977.

24. Grant, "Patristic Evidence," 117.

More pertinently, Eldon J. Epp addressed the matter quite frankly in his article regarding the "Twentieth Century Interlude in New Testament Textual Criticism":

> No theory of the text [exists] which would allow for the establishment of a definitive critical text . . . . *We simply do not have a theory of the text* . . . . No clear and adequate answer is forthcoming . . . . *The lack of a definitive theory and history of the early text and the lack of progress in critical editions has caused . . . a chaotic situation in the evaluation of variant readings in the NT text.* The result has been the almost universal employment of the 'eclectic' method . . . . [Some] seem to assume that the eclectic method is, for all practical purposes, fully legitimated and acceptable and represents a final method, a permanent procedure, while others of us find K. W. Clark's judgment the *only* acceptable assessment of eclecticism . . . . Numerous variant readings become little more than detached pieces of a puzzle which must now be selected entirely on the basis of their shape and fitness for the space to be filled . . . . In short, *eclecticism is a holding action, a temporary and interim method with presumably equally temporary results* . . . . *To be sure, the question of originality is not aided materially by this approach.*[25]

Epp persevered in a follow-up article by asking:

> Where is the methodological advance if our critical text still approximates that of the late nineteenth century or if we still cannot clearly trace its early history? . . . Have we perchance arrived at a text roughly similar in character to that of the past by somehow circumventing the whole methodological question? I would venture the suggestion that *it is more by default than by reason* that our best critical text today bears the image of the best nineteenth-century text . . . . *Where is the substantive advance if . . . we possess no comprehensive and generally accepted theory to support and justify that form of the text? . . . .* We seem to

---

25. Epp, "Twentieth-Century Interlude," 403–405, 398 (emphasis added). For a greatly extended discussion of problems facing eclecticism, see Epp, "Eclectic Method," 211–57.

have been unable to formulate a theory of the NT text that would explain and justify the modern critical text . . . We remain largely in the dark as to how we might reconstruct the textual history that has left . . . numerous pieces of a puzzle that we seem incapable of fitting together. . . . We seem now to have no such theories and no plausible sketches of the early history of the text that are widely accepted . . . . We offer no such theories at all to vindicate our accepted text . . . . [we are] *advocating textual criticism by intuition.*

Some broad text-critical theory ought to be sought to justify the form of the NT text that scholars and exegetes use . . . . not . . . one that disclaims any comprehensive textual theory as its basis and justification except a "local-genealogical" assessment of each variation-unit and the "automatic significance" of the earliest papyri and uncials . . . . We shall want—and I think need—to have something better, something that rests more firmly on the solid rock of historical reconstruction and less upon *the shifting sands of a serviceable but tentative and sometimes slippery eclecticism or of a myopic variant-by-variant assessment, even though it is in the hands of an expert practitioner.*[26]

And yet—despite these cogent declamations against the eclectic method and its (perhaps) unintended results—Epp nevertheless regards the more reasonable positions relating to Byzantine priority as merely "a curious and regrettable retrogression emphasized by a few North American scholars of a conservative theological persuasion."[27]

---

26. Epp, "Continuing Interlude," 137–40, 142, 150–51 (emphasis added).

27. Epp, "Requiem," 95. Yet cf. Stevens, "John 9.38–39," 20: "Textual criticism should not be controlled by one's theological inclination but by a formal and thorough interaction with the physical textual evidence"—a statement that by all accounts should be the mantra for the Byzantine priority theory and praxis.

ECLECTICISM AND RESULTANT ZERO-SUPPORT

In an earlier article, I demonstrated that the NA[27] critical text had at least one hundred and five whole verses whose entire running text as printed did *not* exist in any known MS, version, or patristic writer.[28] This was followed by a subsequent study (yet unpublished) that revealed an additional two hundred and ten *two-verse* segments (beyond the previous one hundred and five!) that in their continuous running text similarly lacked *any* actual existence in MSS, versions, or patristic writers.[29] Obviously, as the number of sequential verses increases, the number of zero-support segments would increase geometrically, with questionable results regarding theological textual confidence as a by-product.[30]

Regarding the zero-support affecting numerous verses not only in the NA edition, but also the UBS and even the ECM editions, this is the net effect of eclectic praxis in general.[31] The result is a non-extant *Ausgangstext* supposedly presumed to underlie the entire manuscript tradition. In light of this resultant disconnect, even Mink's CBGM ultimately falls short of what it supposedly should deliver if intended to have any authority whatever.[32] The results produced by any form of eclecticism or the CBGM method

28. Robinson, "Rule 9," 27–61.

29. Robinson, "*De facto* Conjecture," 14–16.

30. Regarding "a person's lack of theology and geometry," see Reilly, *Blood on their Hands*.

31. Cf. Epp's comment from a differing context: "Contributions to NT textual criticism . . . have been, I dare say, more of a random and piecemeal nature than of a unified or epoch-making kind" (Epp, "Requiem," 96).

32. From the "Summary of Peter Gurry's dissertation," 318–19: "The official explanations [of the CBGM] are often dense and cumbersome . . . Misunderstanding has ensued . . . . [with] subsequent confusion even among the editors of the ECM themselves . . . . The method is practically unnecessary for those who follow the Byzantine priority position even as it challenges key assumptions of thoroughgoing eclecticism . . . . The CBGM's current practice is inconsistent in some . . . cases and excludes valuable data in others . . . . The method can provide no shortcut to determine the cause (let alone a single cause) of variation."

break down as soon as one moves beyond the individual variant unit to a connected sequence of units, the resultant text found even in a small array of variant units becoming textually unique (i.e., without actual manuscript, versional, or patristic support), existing solely in particular printed editions. This implies what Calvin Porter had noted: that modern eclecticism, although:

> not based upon a theory of the history of the text, does reflect a certain presupposition about that history, [namely that] very early the original text was rent piecemeal and so carried to the ends of the earth where the textual critic, like lamenting Isis, must seek it by his skill.[33]

In other words, eclecticism in its ultimate effect sets forth an "original" text that as an entity failed to maintain itself throughout transmissional history. Such an indictment represents the tip of a transmissional iceberg that seriously should call into question *any* likelihood that a text determined eclectically (by whatever means) should represent a putative historical entity. Is this somehow a superior alternative to the theory regarding actual textual transmission and popular recognition as offered by Byzantine priority, or should a wavering speculation transcend a more logical and solid approach?[34] William G. Pierpont addressed this issue in an unpublished essay:

> Because [eclectic] decisions are arbitrary and subjective, there can be no stability or finality established. There becomes a tendency to make a 'game' of textual criticism, a game which is unending—since the subjective nature of it makes for disagreements among various critics—and then it becomes an occupation. Those who trust criticism of this type find only an ever-changing text of Scripture in their hands, and this may make both critic and his readers doubtful as to the integrity of Scripture or to

---

33. Porter, "Textual Analysis," 12. Note also p. 31: "Textual criticism without a history of the text is not possible."

34. These comments reflect matters discussed by email discussion between the present writer and Peter Gurry, April, 2013.

the possibility of its ever being established with certainty. This situation . . . is destructive to all involved.

Trustworthy textual criticism endeavors to take the evidence as it is, resolve each item on the basis of reliable evidence . . . to the degree possible and present it honestly. It will find that the vast majority of discrepancies easily resolve into certainties which need no further examination or study (the work there is done), while a relatively small number must remain unresolved. Only upon those will there be a need for further textual labors to attempt to resolve them. The textual critic should work himself out of a job.

The end point will be a text in which but a few items remain uncertain, and these are clearly stated and admitted. It will be the closest to the autographic text we can claim, ... verifiable by every honest investigator who may wish to check . . . . If the textual critic will approach this task with humility, in full subjection to God, he will avoid the risks and dangers to himself and to those who trust his work. His work will stand honest challenges, and the results will stand on their own feet.[35]

As the thoroughgoing eclectic George D. Kilpatrick noted regarding reasoned eclecticism:

We can go through many comments and find what look like little bits of original composition in imagining reasons why scribes may have done this or that, but for these imaginitive [sic] reconstructions we are given neither evidence nor corroboration . . . . [There is a] tendency to treat each variant in isolation. We can see how a reliance on external evidence can encourage such a tendency . . . . In any case it seems clear that frequently the decisive

---

35. Pierpont, "Textual Criticism," unpublished papers. Pierpont further stated, "I have spent too many years in science-engineering to ignore hard data. I could not be honest with myself or others to neglect such an abundance and confine myself to a few MSS, no matter how 'wisely' chosen, for the choosing would of necessity be founded merely on opinion . . . . If all these are wrong, then we must be at sea, and every man for himself to pick and choose."

voice in [individual] textual decisions is that of external attestation.[36]

Eclectic claims to the contrary reflect an attempt to divert the discussion from transmissional integrity and plausibility for an actual transmissionally based *Ausgangstext*. A posted comment on the now-defunct internet TC-Alternate list summed up the situation admirably:

The three main problems facing NT textual criticism as a discipline today:

1. There is no agreed upon objective and scientific method which operates independently of one's viewpoint of the textual transmission theory.

2. There is no articulated and reliable hierarchy or set of meta-principles which can arbitrate between the "standard canons" of TC when their evidence is conflicting.

3. There is no deterministic and scientific over-arching methodology that can organize, coordinate, and control the two separate but interdependent tasks of reconstructing (a) the text, and (b) the history of transmission.

> Until these three main (and one must say fatal) flaws in NTTC methodology are adequately fixed . . . to replace the broken, partial, uncoordinated and inadequate attempts of the present, NTTC will continue to flounder in the errors of the past. At the same time, the very same problems will also continue to hinder and cripple any real progress toward the reconstruction of the NT text.[37]

In contrast, I suggest that the Byzantine priority hypothesis remains far more plausible on transmissional grounds, even granting that no existing MS prior to the fourth century has an actual Byzantine pattern of readings in the *ca.* 6 percent of the text under discussion (even though numerous Byzantine *readings* exist in that

36. Kilpatrick, "Review," 267–68, 266.
37. Carroll, "Nazaroo."

earlier period—a number greatly increased by including combined variants with both Byzantine/Alexandrian, Byzantine/ Western or Byzantine/Caesarean support). Allowing for such, the text resulting from those combinations will be *far* more Byzantine than one might otherwise imagine—plus the general unity and pattern of readings found in such a text will *exceed* that found among critical texts established on an eclectic basis that lack a demonstrable transmissional consensus (whether NA/UBS, ECM, or CBGM).

WHAT ABOUT THE HARRY STURZ METHOD? [38]

To urge this is not to say that the "Sturzian concept" of following two out of the three major and "local" texttypes (Alexandrian, Western, Byzantine) should be regarded as a solution, even though its resultant text will tend to be far more "Byzantine" save for the small number of instances where the Alexandrian/Western combination stands against the Byzantine. In effect,—the ultimate pitfall of such a method is to enshrine the *least secure,* and *most weakly supported* "Western" text as the highly questionable ultimate determiner regarding textual authenticity.[39] More to the point, Sturz only claimed *equal antiquity* for the Alexandrian, Western, and Byzantine texttypes, but made *no* claim that such two out of three texttype combinations would "restore the presumed autograph"— at best the Sturz method such would produce a set of *readings* that would be *generally familiar* during the second century. As Sturz stated:

> The Byzantine . . . is an independent witness to the second-century tradition *of its locale* . . . . [It] has *undergone editorial treatment,* as have the other text-types . . . . It constitutes an additional, genealogically unrelated witness to *second-century readings,* along with the Western

---

38. See Sturz, *Byzantine Text-Type.*

39. Since the combinations Alexandrian/Byzantine and Western/Byzantine already produce a resultant Byzantine text, it is only the departure of the Western from the Byzantine that in certain variant units would alter the supposedly "preferred" reading.

> and Alexandrian text-types . . . . *It cannot be treated as
> 'primary'* . . . . [but] should be given equal weight, along
> with the Alexandrian and 'Western' texts, in evaluating
> external evidence for readings.[40]

By this standard, the relatively few variants with separate Alexandrian/Western support actually impact *negatively* the otherwise generally unified Byzantine consensus, thereby creating a *less* discernible pattern of readings not to be found in *any* single manuscript, texttype, or general consensus of manuscripts, regardless of the fact that no two manuscripts—even among the Byzantines—will tend to agree *en toto.* Yet any two Byzantine manuscripts will retain a *more stable pattern of readings* despite their minor differences than results from either reasoned or rigorous eclecticism or the Sturzian two-out-of-three texttype approach.[41] Such transmissional stability *cannot* be maintained when a primarily Byzantine type of text becomes disrupted by eclectic choice or by individual Alexandrian/Western readings scattered sporadically throughout the biblical text.

The Sturzian model is further obviated by the current observation that the theory of texttypes associated with geographical location has generally been rejected,[42] replaced by acknowledged textual "clusters" sharing certain patterns of readings to varying degree (even if still termed by the older names), putative geographic location no longer maintaining a central role.[43]

---

40. Sturz, *Byzantine Text-Type,* 128, 130 (emphasis added). See also Sturz, *Second Century.*

41. Grant, "Patristic Evidence," 123, explains the varying eclectic processes in a pithy, down-to-earth manner: "The student is encouraged to count noses when some of the noses belong to cows and others to horses. Only the cows count."

42. Cf. Theophilos, "Authenticity of John 9:38–39a": "There is a distinct shift away from the division of the text into strict text-types in emerging text-critical discussions."

43. Cf. even Miller, *Present State,* 31: "The Western is *not* . . . confined to the West . . . . Western readings are discovered all over the Church of the early times . . . . *The theory of groups . . . fails to provide for innumerable stems of descent existing in a variety of places*" (emphasis added).

The current recognition (held by Wachtel and others, reflected in the CBGM) is that *a single basic text* was consistently transmitted through the centuries, with various deviations into specific loosely framed clusters. The Byzantine priority position has no problem with this approach, regarding the several clusters with minority support as reflective of textual *deviation* from that original basic consensus text.[44] Such a position stands opposed to the current CBGM reconstruction of a purported *Ausgangstext* that mostly conforms to the critical text (even while some dozens of individual readings are altered in favor of the Byzantine).

Although the Byzantine priority hypothesis is often criticized on the ground that its specific *pattern* of readings is not particularly demonstrable among pre-fourth century witnesses, the point remains that the *general pattern* of Byzantine readings *can* be demonstrated in a reasonable consensus among existing pre-fourth century representatives simply by considering Alexandrian/Byzantine and Western/Byzantine readings as part of the overall consensus. Beyond that, after the fourth century, the Byzantine consensus perseveres throughout numerous regions over a span of more than a thousand years. This, even while the pattern of readings displayed among modern critical editions—up to and including the CBGM—cannot be found in *any* manuscript, version, or patristic witness at *any* point in transmissional history. Historical reality should be connected with transmissional reality, and *both* should become a major factor when recognizing and establishing the original text—and that far more than the questionably supported variant patchworks created by means of the diverse eclectic critical approaches.[45]

---

44. Much the same is noted by Miller, *Present State*, 12: "Corruption crept in through natural causes from the earliest period; but the true tradition remained throughout unimpaired . . . . *Nothing short of this will account for and explain the practical unanimity that has existed since the fourth century, . . .* during all of the manuscriptal period of which remains have descended to us" (emphasis added).

45. Miller, *Present State*, 33: "Is the treasure that has descended to us to be mutilated at the order of subjective scholarship, when a system of inferring from definite evidence is in our hands?"

A matter requiring major clarification is the definition of the term "Byzantine priority":[46] the term does *not* involve merely selecting a Byzantine variant in those units where the greater part of the Byzantine MSS are united in a particular point of textual variation—that merely describes the *result* deriving from the theory of Byzantine priority, but is not the *reason* for such. The basis of the term is that the Byzantine Textform is presumed to have an existence *prior* to that of other textual types or clusters. The necessary distinction is that those other types and clusters reflect textual *departures* from the previously existing (and thus "prior") Byzantine Textform itself, whether such departures result from formal recension or by means of a "process."[47] Such a conception clearly opposes the contrary view suggesting the Byzantine to be a *later* product derived from supposed predecessor texttypes or clusters.[48] Once matters are viewed from this perspective, the contrasting

46. This section relates to discussions held between the present writer and Peter Gurry in 2022.

47. Regarding recensional activity, cf. Bruce, *Answers to Questions*, 159. "The Alexandrian text is, in fact, *a text edited* about the beginning of the third century according to the best traditions of Alexandrian philological scholarship" (emphasis added). So also Colwell, "Method in Establishing," 54: "The Beta [Alexandrian] text-type . . . *is a 'made' text*, probably Alexandrian in origin, produced in part by the selection of relatively 'good old MSS.' but more importantly *by the philological know-how of Alexandrians*" (emphasis added). More explicitly, O'Neill, "Rules," 220, 222: "I am more doubtful, however, about the conclusion that the fourth-century Codex Vaticanus is an example of a carefully preserved text and not the result of *deliberate recension*" (220); "They reckoned that their predecessors were more likely to have added than subtracted; and *they aimed for small-scale lucidity*" (222); The conscious decision to . . . 'Prefer the shorter text wherever possible'" (224); "The rule, 'Make pertinent (if difficult) sense always' . . . . a rule that could lead them astray" (225); "*Conscious editing* to produce a text that is lucid (if difficult) at all costs" (227); "We should watch to see that this rule, too, did not lead them to be too neat, too clever" (228) Emphasis added. See also Robinson, "Recensional Nature," 46–74.

48. Cf. Clark, "Manuscripts," 10: "The majority opinion does affirm that the Neutral [Alexandrian] text is at present our closest approach to the original, and that Codex Vaticanus upon which it was chiefly based is to be accorded the first place among all our sources. But it is also recognized that *this may be only a recension which represents early usage in Egypt*" (emphasis added).

insight well illustrates "reasoned transmissionalism" from a true Byzantine priority perspective. As Max Imhof stated in relation to classical Greek literature, a quite different perspective should exist regarding the "initial" or *Ausgangstext* from that presumed by contemporary NT textual theory:

> The textual history of Greek authors always leads via Byzantium, and the Byzantine Textform is the basis of our manuscript tradition and thus the textual level that can initially be reached by comparing manuscripts.[49]

Further, as Ulrich Victor has noted,

> The customary evaluation of manuscripts and manuscript groups according to their assumed quality and value within the tradition *or according to their geographical distribution* on the one hand *ignores the reality of the transmission,* and is on the other hand *not a rationally defensible procedure.*[50]

The historian Barbara Tuchman astutely observed, "Persistence of the normal is usually greater than the effect of disturbance."[51] One should remember that the Byzantine Textform is *not* a monolithic entity, but in effect represents a *general consensus* resulting from comparison of numerous interrelated but otherwise autonomous streams of transmission that maintain separate currency under the "Byzantine" designation. As von Soden noted,[52] these separate **K** [= Κοινη or "common"] streams include at least the particular and differing forms K^1, K^a, K^{ak}, K^x, K^r, K^i, K^{ik}, K^c, as well as the Byzantine or "Antiochian" commentaries A^a, A^b, A^c, etc. (Chrysostom, Victor, and Titus-Bostra).[53]

---

49. Imhof, "Anhang zur Überlieferungsgeschichte," 291 ("Die Texgeschichte griechischer Autoren führt immer über Byzanz, und die byzantinische Textform ist die Grundlage unserer handschriftlichen Tradition und somit diejenige Textstufe, welche mit dem Handschriftenvergleich zunächst zu erreichen ist").

50. Victor, "Textkritischer Kommentar" (emphasis added).

51. Tuchman, *Distant Mirror,* xix.

52. Soden, *Die Schriften,* 712–893.

53. Lake and Lake, "Byzantine Text," 253: "According to him [Von Soden],

Only *after* such clarification regarding individual Byzantine textual streams is grasped can one begin to see how claims regarding "textual absolutism" might be applied to Byzantine priority theory.[54] Given the diverse textual parameters, a consensus-based Byzantine reading derived from those individual transmissional streams would provide a reason to follow such consensus in the vast majority of variant units where a particular reading enjoys almost total support from the documents representing the constituent lines of transmission comprising the Byzantine Textform. Only in that regard does the Byzantine priority theory—in the vast majority of instances—reflect some sort of "textual absolutism," even though such is decidedly *not* the case in the many passages where the MSS comprising the Byzantine Textform are themselves divided to a significant degree.[55] As Kilpatrick noted, "Few or no editors would pretend that they made each decision with equal certainty,"[56] and such is the case even among Byzantine prior-

---

K existed before the IVth century . . . . Its influence can be traced in contaminated mss. in the fifth century or even earlier." The Lakes reject this concept, suggesting that "von Soden's *K* . . . is a figment made up out of the groups of manuscripts which he calls K^l, and K^x and K^r, not a text already in existence" (254). That claim, however, fails to account for the ultimate origin of those three Byzantine streams, and assumes a type of process view: "the *K* groups [arose from] a process of gradual preference for one variant over another . . . [with] no one of them [being] suddenly created" (254). "Simultaneously a text appears which is more standardized than any which preceded it" (155)—but the continued discussion in this essay brings the "process" model into further question; see *infra*. Even the Lakes vitiate their own "process" view by suggesting "The scribes who were responsible for the variations in the Byzantine text introduced *relatively few and unimportant changes,* they shunned all originality" (257, emphasis added).

54. Lake and Lake, "Byzantine Text," 252: "What we have called the 'Byzantine' texts, . . . for there were several texts, not one." Cf. Colwell, *Best New Testament*, 70: "From the tenth to the fourteenth centuries at least four distinguishable revisions of this Greek Vulgate were produced."

55. For the purposes of understanding, a "significant degree" of division among the Byzantine MSS can range from a near-equal 50 percent-50 percent division down to an approximate 70 percent-30 percent division, with preference generally tending toward the majority consensus as the level of opposing Byzantine support declines.

56. Kilpatrick, "Review," 262.

ity practitioners. As one comment on the Puritan Board blogsite noted:

> There is at least a reasonable case for preferring texts which were commonly used in the church, and carefully studying, weighting, and collating them. Not that you would just take a statistical approach, but weight that type of text more heavily.[57]

REGARDING THE "PROCESS" VIEW

As for the "process" view in general (championed early on by Colwell[58] and currently advocated by Klaus Wachtel),[59] the idea is not new. S. W. Whitney basically described the concept in the 1890s:

> The plea [of critical text editors] . . . is, that between the first and the tenth or twelfth century changes were gradually introduced until the text became so largely corrupted as to need to be corrected by returning to the readings found in the oldest manuscripts, versions, and Fathers.[60]

Yet the primary problem with the process remains what Zane Hodges described in various articles since 1968:

> No one has yet explained how a long, slow process spread out over many centuries as well as over a wide geographical area, and involving a multitude of copyists, who often knew nothing of the state of the text outside of their own monasteries or scriptoria, could achieve this widespread uniformity out of the diversity presented by the earlier

57. West, "Inadequate View," #254.

58. Colwell, *Best New Testament,* 64: "It is more accurate to regard a text-type as a process than as a single event"; Colwell, "Method in Establishing," 53: "A text-type is a process, not the work of one hand."

59. Cf. Wachtel, "Discussion," 6: "The manuscript tradition of the New Testament is a very consistent one. As a result of quantitative and genealogical analysis a structure emerges which can best be described in terms of *gradual change or continuous development*" (emphasis added).

60. Whitney, *Revisers' Greek Text,* 1:15–16.

forms of text. Even an official edition of the New Testament—promoted with ecclesiastical sanction throughout the known world—would have had great difficulty achieving this result as the history of Jerome's Vulgate amply demonstrates. But an unguided process achieving relative stability and uniformity in the diversified textual, historical, and cultural circumstances in which the New Testament was copied, imposes impossible strains on our imagination.[61]

As minor as most textual differences might appear in the average unit of variation, it remains difficult to comprehend how a "process" could have displaced numerous sequential readings from an Alexandrian/critical text base to that of the Byzantine Textform or vice versa. For example, it would be extremely difficult for an unguided "process" to result in the numerous differentiated readings considered in sequence within various verses such as the following:

Matthew 11:23, Nestle-Aland critical text and the Byzantine Textform (𝔐), with differences underlined:[62]

NA   καɩ συ Καφαρναουμ, μηεως ουρανου υψωθηση; εως Αɩδου

𝔐   καɩ συ Καπερναοθμ ηεως τουουρανου υψωθεɩσα; εως Αɩδου

NA   And you, Capharnaum, not unto heaven will you be exalted? Unto Hades

𝔐   And you, Capernaum, the one unto heaven having been exalted? Unto Hades

NA   καταβησηοτι εɩ εν Σοδομοɩς εγενηθησαν αɩ δυναμεɩς

𝔐   καταβιβασθηση οτι εɩ εν Σοδομοɩς εγενοντο αɩ δυναμεɩσ

---

61. Hodges, "Greek Text," 334–345; Hodges, "Defense"; Hodges and Hodges, "Appendix C," 175.

62. For the record, the 𝔐 parallel at Lk 10:15, while agreeing with 𝔐 in Matthew regarding καɩ συ . . . καταβιβασθηση, *lacks* the remainder of the verse—an unlikely situation were harmonization to the parallel in view. Further, NA in Luke 10:15 reads identically to NA in Mt *except* for adding του before Αδου.

NA   you will <u>descend</u>. Because if in Sodom <u>had been occurring</u> the powers

𝔐   you will <u>be descending</u>. Because if in Sodom <u>occurred</u> the powers

NA   αι γενομεναι εν σοι, <u>εμεινεν</u> αν μεχρι της σημερον.

𝔐   αι γενομεναι εν σοι, <u>εμειναν</u> αν μεχρι της σημερον.

NA   having been done in you, <u>it</u> would have remained until today.

𝔐   having been done in you, <u>they</u> would have remained until today.

So also Matt 15:35–36, where once more it becomes difficult to see an unguided "process" resulting in the sequence of underlined altered variants in both NA and 𝔐:

NA   και <u>παραλλειλας</u> <u>τω οχλω</u> αναπεσειν επι την γην, <u>ελαβεν</u>

𝔐   και <u>εκελευσεν</u> <u>τοις εχλοις</u> αναπεσειν την γην, <u>και λαβων</u>

NA   And <u>having commanded</u> the <u>crowd</u> to recline upon the ground, <u>he took</u>

𝔐   And <u>he instructed</u> the <u>crowds</u> to recline upon the ground, <u>and having taken</u>

NA   τους επτα αρτοθς και τους ιχθυας <u>και</u> ευχαριστησας εκλασεν και <u>εδιδου</u>

𝔐   τους επτα αρτους και τους ιχθυας ευχαριστησας εκλασεν και <u>εδωκεν</u>

NA   the seven loaves and the fishes, <u>and</u> having given thanks, he broke and <u>was giving</u>

𝔐   the seven loaves and the fishes, having given thanks, he broke and <u>gave</u>

NA   τοις μαθηταις οι δε μαθηται <u>τοις οχλοις</u>.

𝔐   τοις μαθηταις <u>αυτου</u>, οι δε μαθηται <u>τω οχλω</u>.

NA   to <u>the</u> disciples and the disciples to <u>the crowds</u>

𝔐   to <u>his</u> disciples and the disciples to the <u>crowd</u>

In contrast, it is very easy to see various "processes" or recensional activity at work in regard to the production of deviating minority readings, resulting in textual clusters that differing from a dominant original form of the text, but failing to achieve transmissional ascendency (a situation that, according to Westcott and Hort, would require not only a formal recension process, but also a high level of ecclesiastical approval, support, and promulgation).[63] Wachtel of course is correct in presuming a single basic text that has been transmitted consistently through the centuries, with various deviations occurring that form specific textual clusters—he simply ignores the further implications that would point to that original text having held some sort of dominance from the very first (which is what Westcott and Hort had suggested would happen, absent a formal recension occurrence at a later date).[64]

CONCLUDING THOUGHTS

To close this discussion, I offer three interesting and important observations, the first from Kenneth W. Clark:

> The Bible is for us the word of God, our chief guide for the salvation of humanity. . . . The Bible is the historic basis for the Christian religion, and we who are Christians

---

63. Lake and Lake, "Byzantine Text," 253: "It might seem to imply that the [Byzantine] text was officially recognized, which is not the case."

64. To reiterate (cf. note 14 above): "A majority of extant documents is more likely to reflect a majority of ancestral documents *at each stage of transmission* than *vice versa*." (Westcott and Hort, *Introduction*, 45, emphasis added). Allowing for their "Byzantine recension" hypothesis, this situation was exemplified by the domination of the Byzantine text from its supposed fourth century origin until the invention of printing: "Before the close of the fourth century, . . . a Greek text not materially differing from the almost universal text of the ninth century and the Middle Ages *was dominant*, probably by authority . . . . The text which finally emerged triumphant in the East was *not* a result of any such process, in which the Antiochian [Byzantine] text would have been but one factor, however considerable" (Westcott and Hort, "Introduction," 142, emphasis added).

perceive in it, above all other writings, man's only hope of life. It is with this book that the textual critic deals. This is the book whose true text he seeks, and whose transmission from generation to generation he studies to understand.[65]

Next, a most insightful comment written *ca.* 1977 from my Greek NT co-editor, William G. Pierpont:

> The Majority/Traditional/Consensus Text position is the only fully defensible position. It can stand on its own feet, and appears to be in full accord with Divine Providence and the laws of Scriptural Evidence. It requires no dogmatic assertions, no astute scholarly proclamations, no pleas for extra-documentary sources or criteria. Prejudices and human opinions are excluded. It rests its case on the open, obvious, clear facts alone. It is completely logical, and in the purer sense is absolutely "scientific".[66]

Finally, it is most appropriate to quote a prayer from Westcott regarding "a devout reverence of God's Word":

> Blessed Lord, by Whose Providence all Holy Scriptures were written and preserved for our instruction, give us grace to study them each day with patience and love. Strengthen our souls with the fulness of their divine teaching. Keep from us all pride and irreverence. Guide us in the deep things of Thy heavenly wisdom; and, of Thy great mercy, lead us by Thy Word into everlasting life, through Jesus Christ our Saviour. *Amen.*[67]

---

65. Clark, "Manuscripts," 1.

66. Pierpont, unpublished document found among his many files.

67. Westcott, "Devout Reverence," 420.

Chapter 4

A STURZIAN SOLUTION TO THE PROBLEM OF "ORIGINAL TEXT" AS ILLUSTRATED BY EPH 1:1, MATT 5:22, AND JOHN 3:13

DAVID ALAN BLACK

INTRODUCTION

The aim of this chapter is that of William Tyndale—"To cause the plowboy to know the Scriptures."[1] Like my previous publications, *New Testament Textual Criticism: A Concise Guide* and *Rethinking New Testament Textual Criticism*, this chapter attempts to make the findings of scholarship available to a wide readership. There is nothing I love more than writing for a general audience and taking the deeper things of God and attempting to make them plain for everyday readers. The great A. T. Robertson once called the Greek New Testament "the Torchbearer of Light and Progress for the

---

1 *Foxe's Book of Martyrs*, 169.

world."[2] If this is true (and it is), then any light we can shed *on* the text of the New Testament ought to help us gain light *from* it. Textual criticism is an intricate and demanding field of study, but it is not an impossible field, even for beginners. The Bible was given to reveal truth, not obscure it. God surely intends that we understand it. Hence, understanding the Bible is vital because our doctrines of God, man, salvation, and future things (to name but four) rest on a correct hermeneutic. Every word of Scripture is worthy of the reader's sweat.

In this chapter I intend to show, in contrast to both reasoned eclecticism and the Byzantine priority position, that the Byzantine text type is neither primary nor secondary but a useful and independent witness to the text of the New Testament in that it is neither edited nor secondary in the Westcott-Hort sense. My views are largely, though not exclusively, based on the work of my former teacher and colleague in the Greek department at Biola University, Dr. Harry Sturz. For many years, Sturz's views were sorely neglected by scholars. However, with the reprint of his 1967 doctoral dissertation, one may hope that this situation will change.[3] Many scholars have insisted that the Byzantine text, though it may occasionally contain a reading that could be valuable for the purposes of textual criticism, is vastly inferior to the Alexandrian text. Other scholars, clearly in the minority, have argued for the priority, primacy, or even exclusivity of the Byzantine text. In my opinion, the most optimal view is a mediating position that avoids both extremes.

During my seminary days at Talbot School of Theology and well into my own teaching career, I adhered to reasoned eclecticism. My Talbot professors all espoused this view. As I recall, very little was said in our classes about New Testament textual criticism. The consensus view was the consensus view, and all one needed to do was follow the reading printed above the line in the

---

2. Robertson, *Minister*, 116.

3. Sturz, *Byzantine Text-Type*. Since Sturz himself did not give a label to his view (e.g., independent text-type theory, equitable eclecticism, reasoned transmissionalism, etc.), I have refrained from doing so in this chapter.

United Bible Societies' *Greek New Testament*. Over time, however, the perspective of Harry Sturz began to stick to me like a gadfly in ointment. Sturz presented evidence that Byzantine readings are supported by early papyri and concluded that, since the Byzantine text was not edited in the Westcott-Hort sense of the term, they derive from at least the second century and represent a stream of tradition independent of other early traditions. Prior to the work of Sturz, Gunther Zuntz had made a similar claim regarding Byzantine readings. Sturz also agreed with George Kilpatrick and E. C. Colwell (with whom he had worked at Claremont Graduate School) that all viable readings that have enjoyed continuous transmission over the centuries were probably in existence prior to AD 200. In short, Sturz argued that the Byzantine text has very ancient origins that push well back into the beginning of the second century.

During the 2022 Clearview Apologetics Conference, Peter Gurry and Maurice Robinson presented robust arguments for reasoned eclecticism and Byzantine priority respectively. In this chapter, I offer a *tertium quid*, which, while valuing the Alexandrian and Byzantine texts (as well as the Western text), takes a different tack based on the supposition of the independence of all three of these text types.[4] If this independence can be established—again, you will have to read Sturz for the arguments—then the reading found in the majority of text types is, all things being equal, the most likely to be the original one.[5]

---

4. Today there is considerable skepticism about whether one should still speak of "text types." I am reluctant to jettison the term. I tend to agree with Eldon Epp when he writes that ". . . it seems clear to me that the grouping of early witnesses is possible (and such groups or clusters might very well be designated 'text-types')." On the same page he adds, "Much more work, admittedly, is required in this area, but we should not so easily capitulate to those forces that contend that no text-type existed or can be easily identified in the pre-fourth century period of NT textual transmission." See Epp, "Textual Criticism," 99.

5. It should be noted that Sturz claimed no more than to be able to recover the text of the second century. It is my own conviction, not his necessarily, that these consensus readings also push back into the first century and thus have a claim to originality.

In the remainder of this chapter, I shall attempt to expand on the Sturzian theory of Byzantine independence and usefulness (but not priority) by offering three examples of textual variations based on my previous publications. Before I begin, however, I should like to make three points clear. The first is that each of the conference speakers, despite our differences, share the same high theology. We all view the New Testament as inspired, infallible, and inerrant in the autographs. Our divisions should never be discussed except in the context of this mutual affirmation.

In the second place, each of us would gladly acknowledge that we have not lost a single word of the New Testament. The text of the New Testament is, in fact, solidly established in at least 96 percent of its contents—a higher percentage (99 percent) if one concludes that there are only about two thousand significant variants in the New Testament, a number I argue for in my book *New Testament Textual Criticism*.

Finally, you, the reader, must decide how important this subject is to you. One of the things Christians disagree about is the importance of their disagreements. The clear danger is that we make too much of textual criticism on the one hand, or we make too little of it on the other. In this chapter I will argue for the originality of readings that most reasoned eclectics have rejected. I believe these scholars are wrong and will try to persuade you of such. But it is far better that you take up the task for yourself, always keeping in mind that, generally speaking, the original reading will be found either above or below the line in our printed Greek New Testaments, or either in the text or footnotes of our English Bible translations.

In my M.Div. thesis at Talbot, I had an opportunity to apply the Sturzian approach to the famous variant in Eph 1:1. I argued on the basis of both the external evidence and the internal evidence that the words ἐν Ἐφέσῳ were in fact original and that Paul had primitively sent the letter to the believers in Ephesus. Later, as a student in New Testament at the University of Basel, I had the opportunity to publish my findings in a journal article.[6]

6. Black, "Peculiarities," 59–73.

This was the first olive in the jar, and once it was removed, other essays on textual criticism followed easily. In my forty-six years of teaching Greek, I have tried to guard against the notion that only scholars can understand the field of New Testament textual criticism. For that reason, I have tried to produce written materials whose purpose is to elucidate for all Christians how to go about doing textual criticism in general and how to resolve variants for themselves. I hope and pray that this chapter might have the same impact. Because it is based on my oral presentation at the Clearview Apologetics Conference, I have tried to reproduce here my more conversational style—a kind of hybrid, if you will, between speaking and writing. Those wishing a more technical discussion of these matters can consult my other works on the subject.

EXAMPLES OF A STURZIAN SOLUTION

Let us now advance to a discussion of the three major textual variants I focused on in my presentation at the Clearview Apologetics Conference. The first is Eph 1:1. Are the words "in Ephesus" original or not? Here the external evidence seems to favor the inclusion of the disputed words—the reading is both early and widespread: it is supported by both the Byzantine and Western text types.[7] Why, then, would anyone want to omit the words? One possibility is that a scribe excised the words in order to make the letter a universal writing, intended for the church at large rather than for a specific congregation. Scholarship has shown that the early church struggled with the particularity of the Pauline epistles. The issue was, "How can we read a letter as applicable to our situation when that letter was originally written for and sent to another church?" The easiest way to resolve this problem was to omit any reference to a

---

7. In his magisterial commentary on Ephesians, Harold Hoehner argues for the originality of "in Ephesus" because "the geographical distribution of the witnesses that agree in support of the omission of ἐν Ἐφέσῳ is poor, being limited to the Alexandrian text-type, whereas the geographical distribution supporting its inclusion is excellent, being represented by all text-types" (*Ephesians*, 146).

place name in the prescript.[8] The same phenomenon can be seen in Rom 1:7, 15, where the words "in Rome" are omitted in some manuscripts. Later, when the Pauline letters came to be regarded as Scripture to be read and used by all, this somewhat mechanical way of resolving the problem disappeared.

The second variant comes from Matt 5:22.[9] The manuscript evidence allows two possibilities: "If anyone gets angry with his brother," or "If anyone gets angry with his brother without a cause." First, one could argue that the word εἰκῇ ("without a cause") was added to Jesus' statement. This is precisely the argument of Bruce Metzger, speaking for the committee that edited the United Bible Societies' *Greek New Testament*: "Although the reading with εἰκῇ is widespread from the second century onwards, it is much more likely that the word was added by copyists in order to soften the rigor of the precept, than omitted as unnecessary."[10] Along the same lines, Don Carson writes:

> Several observations are in order. First, some early manuscripts of the New Testament add the words "without cause" after "angry with his brother": "But I tell you that anyone who is angry with his brother *without cause* will be subject to judgment." These words are almost certainly a later addition. Some scribe no doubt thought Jesus couldn't possibly have been so rigid as to exclude all anger, and inserted the words to soften the statement.[11]

In other words, a scribe thought Jesus was being too rigid and so inserted the word to soften the statement.

However, the internal evidence may be understood in a different way. While it is true that Jesus' usual method of teaching was expressed in absolute and categorical terms, he sometimes laid down important qualifications in his teachings. In the same chapter of Matthew, Jesus states that his followers are blessed when people utter evil against them "falsely" (5:11). Here the verbal persecution

8. See Dahl, "Particularity," 261–71.

9. See Black, "Jesus on Anger," 1–8

10. Metzger, *Textual Commentary*, 11.

11. Carson, *Sermon on the Mount*, 42–43.

is limited to what is produced "by lying" about the character of the disciples. Neither Jesus nor Peter (1 Pet 3:13–17) was under the delusion that Christian suffering was always for doing good. Hence it is possible that the shorter reading (minus the word εἰκῇ) in 5:22 is an erroneous "improvement" of the text intended to make *all* anger reprehensible. A scribe may have expunged the word εἰκῇ from his copy because he thought it was liable to be understood in a sense too indulgent to anger. Consequently, the internal evidence, as is so often the case, seems inconclusive. Yet another "qualification" of Jesus' teaching in the Matthean Sermon on the Mount is found in Matt 5:32, where Jesus includes the famous exception clause "except for fornication" (found neither in Mark nor Luke).

Looking now at the external evidence (see table below), we see the shorter text has impressive support, mostly Alexandrian (p[67] Aleph, B, Vulgate). It competes, however, with a reading that is equally early and yet more widespread in its attestation. Behind the reading εἰκῇ are manuscripts of the Western, Byzantine, and Alexandrian text types (as well as the "Caesarean" family of witnesses), while the omission of εἰκῇ is supported almost exclusively by witnesses representing one locality (Egypt). Here the question of the relative weight to be given to the Byzantine text comes into play, as does the question of the relative merit of the Alexandrian text type. In this case, external criteria seem to argue that the more widespread reading εἰκῇ has an edge over its more limited alternative.

*Witnesses to the Text of Matt 5:22 by Text Type**

	Byzantine	Western	Alexandrian	"Caesarean"
αὐτοῦ	1292	it[aur] **vg** Tertullian[vid] Augustine[3/4]	𝔓[64]א* **B** **Origen** eth[ms]	

αὐτοῦ εἰκῇ	W Δ 180 597 1006 1010 *Byz* [Ε Σ] *Lect* Chrysostom Basil Theodoret	**D it** vg[mss] syr[s,c,h] Augustine[1/4] Cyprian Hilary Lucifer **Irenaeus**[lat]	[2] ℵ **L** 33 579 1241 cop[sa,] [meg, bo] eth[TH]	Θ *f*[1] *f*[3] 28 157 **565 700** 1071 syr[pal] arm geo Eusebius Cyril

*Important witnesses in bold

The last problem involving textual variation we will focus on occurs in John 3:13.[12] The NIV renders the verse as follows: "No one has ever gone into heaven except the one who came from heaven— the Son of Man." The margin indicates that some manuscripts add "who is in heaven" after the words "the Son of Man." This is an important variant, as it has significance for New Testament Christology. Did Jesus claim to be in heaven while talking to Nicodemus in Jerusalem?

The external evidence may be summarized as follows:

1. The omission of "who is in heaven" is supported by a relatively small number of witnesses. This minority, however, comprises manuscripts generally considered to be of the highest quality—the fourth-century uncials Sinaiticus (Aleph) and Vaticanus (B). On the other hand, this reading is supported by a single text type, the Alexandrian.

2. The inclusion of "who is in heaven" is supported by nearly all the uncial and minuscule manuscripts of the New Testament extant in this portion of John, as well as by nearly every ancient version. In addition, the longer reading is supported by the great majority of the earliest patristic witnesses, including the Alexandrian father Origen. In short, the reading "who is in heaven" was accepted as genuine over a wide geographical area, encompassing most of the then-ancient world: Rome and the West, Greece, Syria and Palestine, and even Alexandria itself (where its omission also was known).

12. See Black, "Text of John 3:13," 49–66.

The following table displays the evidence from the manuscripts, versions, and fathers that have been accumulated and segregated under the leading text types or groups of witnesses:

Witnesses to the Text of John 3:13

Byzantine	Alexandrian	Western	"Caesarean"
(1) ἀνθρώπου ὁ ὢν ἐν τῷ οὐρανῷ A [*vid] (omit ὢν) A[c]EFGHKMSU V ΓΛΠΨ 050 063 (θεοῦ for ἀνθρώπου) 1195 1344 1646 *Byz Lect* Eustathius Aphraates Epiphanius Basil Amphilochius Didymus Chrysostom Nonnus Theodoret	892 cop[bo mss] Origen[lat] Dionysius	It[a,aur,b,c,f,ff2,j,l,q,r2]vg Syr[h] Diatessaron[a] Hippolytus Novatian Hillary Lucifer	Θ *f¹ f³* 28 565 arm geo Cyril
(2) omit	p[66, 75] אBLT[b] W[supp] 083 086 0113 33 1241[copsa,bo mss,ach 2, fay]eth Origen[lat] Didymus	Diatessaron[caarm,v]	Apollinaris Cyril
(3) ὃς ἦν ἐν τῷ οὐρανῷ		it[c]syr[c]	
(4) ὁ ὢν ἐκ τοῦ οὐρανοῦ		0141 80 syr[s]	

On the basis of the external evidence, then, it appears the longer reading is to be preferred. But what about the internal evidence? Let us examine some of the criteria for how to approach such decisions.

Prefer the More Difficult Reading

Preference for the longer reading established on the basis of the external evidence finds strong internal support from this principle, since the longer reading is obviously the more difficult one. It has Christ saying that he was at the moment present both in heaven and on earth while talking with Nicodemus. The awkwardness of this saying explains the omission of the words "who is in heaven," as well as the origin of the two other minor variants in this verse: "who was in heaven" and "who is from heaven."

Prefer the Shorter Reading

Because scribes were sometimes prone to add words, the shorter reading is often preferred. This fact, coupled with the assumed quality of the external evidence, was no doubt crucial in the decision by the editors of the United Bible Societies' *Greek New Testament* to relegate the words "who is in heaven" to the apparatus. However, this principle states that the shorter reading is to be preferred *unless* the scribe either accidentally omitted material or else intentionally omitted material on stylistic, grammatical, or doctrinal grounds. Therefore, although the longer reading may indeed reflect later Christological development, it is also possible the words were found objectionable or superfluous and omitted on that basis. In view of this possibility, the longer reading deserves serious consideration even on the basis of this (disputed) principle of textual criticism.

Prefer the Verbally Dissident Reading

Some scholars have argued that the words "who is in heaven" were added on the model of John 1:18: "No one has ever seen God, but God the One and Only, who is at the Father's side, has made him known." However, the statement in 1:18 is neither directly parallel with 3:13 nor does it belong to the same historical context as the discourse in John 3. It seems this "parallel" is not a true parallel at all.

Prefer the Reading that Best Accounts for the Others

Had the readings "who was in heaven" or "who is from heaven" been original, there is no reason why a scribe would have altered the text. If, however, the longer text is original, one can easily understand the other variants as attempts to modify or, in the case of the shorter text, to remove altogether a difficult expression.

There now remains the matter of what the author was more likely to have written. In this regard one must consider (1) a reading's harmony with the author's teaching elsewhere, and (2) a reading's harmony with the author's style and vocabulary.

The Author's Theology

It is true that the longer reading represents a high Christology. Did John share such a view? The answer is plain: the Johannine Jesus is not only the preexistent Word (1:1) and the post-resurrection exalted Christ (20:28), but also the Revealer who remained "with God" while present on earth (1:1, 14). John's Jesus did not cease to be what he was before the incarnation, for the flesh assumed by the Word was the "tabernacle" in which God was pleased to dwell (1:14). Thus the words "who is in heaven" fit perfectly into the pattern of Johannine Christology.

The Author's Style

A general knowledge of an author's style often will help determine whether a particular variant reading is in harmony with the rest of the author's writings. A check of a Greek concordance reveals that the clause "who is in heaven" faithfully reflects characteristics of Johannine style, grammar, and vocabulary. Six of the eleven occurrences of the participle "who is" with a prepositional phrase appear in the Fourth Gospel (1:18; 3:31; 6:47; 8:47; 12:17; 18:37). Elsewhere, the construction appears only in Matt 12:30; Luke 11:23; Rom 9:5; 2 Cor 11:31; and Eph 2:4. It appears this usage is not only Johannine but almost exclusively so in the New Testament. Hence there is no linguistic evidence why John could not have written these words, and, indeed, he is given over to the repetition of such a construction.

In summary, although much can be said for certain arguments in favor of the shorter reading in John 3:13, the inclusion of the disputed words appears to be the best solution since it is supported by significant external and internal evidence and since it retains a great deal of John's original use of the term "Son of Man." Therefore, this witness to Christ's deity, on our reading of the evidence, is not a mere dogma handed down by the church but it is a witness deriving from Jesus himself, from his own teaching about himself, and verified by John the apostle. His record is that the Son of Man, who has come down from heaven, speaks truthfully about heavenly realities as a man speaks about his own home, for the incarnation did not—indeed could not—denude heaven of the Son's presence.

STURZ'S APPROACH COMPARED TO OTHER APPROACHES

We have discussed but three examples out of many instances of textual variation in the Greek New Testament. Each illustrates a Sturzian solution to the task. In the remainder of this chapter, I should like to spend a few paragraphs comparing the Sturzian view with the other main approaches to New Testament textual criticism, namely rigorous eclecticism, reasoned eclecticism, and Byzantine priority. In several ways the Sturzian view reveals remarkable similarities with all three of these approaches, while at the same time reflecting important differences.

Let us begin with rigorous (thoroughgoing) eclecticism. This approach places primary (if not exclusive) emphasis on the internal evidence. For a reasoned eclectic, the external evidence is essential but mostly because it serves as a repository for readings. Once the Greek manuscripts—and, to a lesser extent, the ancient versions and the patristic citations—have given us the variants, the internal evidence kicks in and becomes determinative. In other words, in rigorous eclecticism both the external and the internal evidence are essential, but in dramatically different ways. The external evidence tells us which readings are possible. The internal evidence decides the case. At no time, however, is the external evidence itself capable of resolving the issue. This is largely due to the fact that, for the reasoned eclectic, no single text type or grouping of manuscripts is preferred. The original reading is just as likely to be found in the Byzantine text as in the Alexandrian or Western texts.

Similarly, a Sturzian position eschews any notion of "best" text type or cluster of Greek witnesses. The original reading may be found in every one of the three major text types. Preference is given neither to the Alexandrian text (as is often the case with reasoned eclecticism) nor to the Byzantine text (as is the case with Byzantine priority). Thus Sturz's approach to textual criticism and rigorous eclecticism share a supremely important tenet of textual criticism, namely that the original text cannot be equated with any manuscript or text type.

That said, the Sturzian position, while employing internal evidence as an essential step in determining the original text, insists that the internal evidence by itself is never probative due to its inherent subjectivity. To return for a moment to the text of Matt 5:22, here we see that the external evidence allows for two readings. Either we will include the words "without a cause" or exclude them. From this point forward, the rigorous eclectic will argue for the originality of one or the other reading based solely on the tenets of internal evidence, asking "Which is the more difficult reading?" or "Which reading best comports with the authors' style and/or theology?" and so forth.

Now, a Sturzian approach asks the exact same kinds of questions but finds the internal evidence a bit too "slippery" to be relied upon exclusively. Could "without a cause" be original here? Yes indeed. And a scribe might well have omitted the expression in order to make Jesus' teaching on anger more rigorous. On the other hand, could the original text of Matt 5:22 have lacked εἰκῇ and a later scribe added it in order to soften Jesus' teaching? Absolutely. Here a Sturzian would argue that both readings have a case for originality. Indeed, whenever I teach this passage in my classes I always indicate to my students that both readings are possible based on the internal evidence. I try to avoid a one-sided evaluation of the internal evidence. However, as we have seen, this is not always the case when reading Metzger's *Textual Commentary* or when perusing the commentaries on this verse. We saw how both Metzger and Carson insisted that the words "without a cause" were added to the text in order to soften Jesus' pronouncement on anger—with very little attempt to show that the internal evidence could also support the opposite conclusion. In fact, as I hope to have shown above, the inclusion of εἰκῇ seems to comport far better with the context of the Matthean Sermon on the Mount than does its omission. We noted the "exceptional" nature of the reading εἰκῇ and compared it to other exceptions such as the "falsely" of Matt 5:10 and the "except for fornication" in Matt 5:32. But let me be clear: For a Sturzian, the internal evidence just discussed can hardly be said to "prove" the originality of εἰκῇ. At best we might say that the internal evidence corroborates the reading already established on the basis of the external evidence—namely, that εἰκῇ has a much wider geographical distribution among the major text types.

In summary, then, rigorous eclecticism finds both the external and the internal evidence essential to the task of textual criticism. For a rigorous eclectic, however, the external evidence is never probative. Certainty must be established only based on the internal evidence. It is thought that by so doing, the textual critic can avoid a blind preference for any manuscript or group of manuscripts. The Sturzian position likewise holds both the external and the internal evidence to be indispensable. For a Sturzian, however, and in stark contrast to the rigorous eclectic, the internal evidence is never probative because it is, quite frankly, too subjective. Certainty must therefore be deduced based on the external evidence alone. The one thing that both Sturzian and rigorous eclectics agree upon is that no automatic preference should be given to any one text type.

Let us now move to a comparison of the Sturzian position with reasoned eclecticism. In reasoned eclecticism, both the external and internal evidence are indispensable. The Greek manuscripts are far more than mere safe deposit boxes for readings. They are to be studied for their history, their provenance, their antiquity, their relative trustworthiness, and such like. Internal evidence is then used alongside this external evidence. Sometimes readings that are thought to be original on the basis of the external evidence will be rejected after a closer look at the internal evidence.

Reasoned eclecticism, as pointed out at the Clearview Apologetics Conference, holds sway among the great majority of New Testament textual scholars today. It is reflected in the vast majority of printed editions of the Greek New Testament and in the overwhelming majority of modern English translations of the New Testament (ESV, CSB, NASB, NRSV, etc.). I think it is safe to say that most of the printed editions of the Greek New Testament, as well as the preponderance of English versions, reflect a text that is basically Alexandrian in nature, though no reasoned eclectic that I know would insist that the Alexandrian text type is to be followed slavishly or automatically in places of variation. This is because pride of place is often given by reasoned eclectics to the internal evidence. Some of them (Harold Greenlee, for example) actually prefer to begin their investigations with the internal evidence before even looking at the external evidence. For them, the internal evidence is the starting point of the text-critical task.[13]

What, then, does a Sturzian view have in common with reasoned eclecticism? Much in every way. For one thing, reasoned eclecticism shares a commitment—and I mean a genuine commitment—to take both kinds of evidence, the external as well as the

---

13. For example, Dan Wallace, in an interview with Peter Gurry, confessed to being a Sturzian for a decade and half, but said that it was his study of the *internal* evidence that eroded his confidence in the Sturzian position and led him to espouse reasoned eclecticism instead.

internal, seriously and purposefully. For another thing, reasoned eclecticism claims that no single text type, including the Alexandrian, is to be unquestionably preferred in places of textual variation. We might, in fact, say that a Sturzian position is a version of reasoned eclecticism. Where it differs from reasoned eclecticism is that it insists that the external evidence must always have pride of place. The external evidence, for a Sturzian, is probative; the internal evidence is merely corroborative. In contrast, for a reasoned eclectic, both kinds of evidence might be determinative. In one passage the external evidence might cast the deciding vote, while in another passage the internal evidence serves to function in this way. Even a casual perusal of Metzger's *Textual Commentary* will reveal this approach. Here you will often find a comment like, "The external evidence favors the longer reading here, but the internal evidence seems to contradict it. The committee, therefore, preferred the shorter reading." You will recall what Metzger said about Matt 5:22 (see above): "Although the reading with εἰκῇ is widespread from the second century onwards, it is much more likely that the word was added by copyists in order to soften the rigor of the precept, than omitted as unnecessary." The result is (often) a preference for the reading supported by the Alexandrian text type.

Again, I should like to make it clear that I am not claiming that reasoned eclectics set out to favor an Alexandrian reading. I do not believe that to be the case. An attempt is genuinely made to allow other text types (including the Byzantine) to accurately reflect the original. That being said, I think it is evident that reasoned eclecticism often ends up preferring an Alexandrian reading, whether consciously or not. It is a preference that is probably completely unconscious and is perhaps due to the residual effects of the Westcott-Hort theory.[14] At this point I want to mention an

14. In the most recent issue of *Filologia Neotestamentaria*, Peter Rodgers opens his essay with the following words: "One of the clear results of the study of New Testament Textual Criticism is the confidence among scholars in the superiority and priority of the Alexandrian text." He adds, "Since Westcott and Hort published their landmark edition, *The New Testament in the Original Greek* in 1881, most scholars have considered the Alexandrian text type to be

important (though often overlooked) study that was published in 1997. The book is called *Textual Optimism: A Critique of the United Bible Societies' Greek New Testament*.[15] Here the author compares the five editions of the United Bible Societies' *Greek New Testament* that had appeared since 1966. His focus is on the textual apparatus and especially the rating system used by the editors to indicate probability of originality. This probability is indicated by a system of letter-ratings (A, B, C, and D). He shows how a considerable amount of "grade inflation" occurred with the publication of the fourth edition, implying a higher degree of certainty than previous editions even though no textual decision had been reversed by the editors. In other words, although there were no changes made in the actual text of the fourth edition, the confidence of the editors in the correctness of their decisions only seemed to become stronger. It does not surprise me, then, that some refer to the United Bible Society's *Greek New Testament* (and its counterpart the Nestle-Aland text) as a "New Standard Text." This is substantiated by the rising number of "A" and "B" ratings and the decline in the number of "C" and "D" ratings. As I said at the beginning of this chapter, when I was in seminary I was essentially told that I could confidently follow the reading printed above the line in my United Bible Society's *Greek New Testament* and would therefore not need trouble myself with exploring the alternatives printed below the line.

Finally, let us examine how a Sturzian position might compare with Byzantine priority. I would like to make two points. First, it is vitally important that we do not lump together these two approaches to textual criticism, as if they had the same position regarding the Byzantine text or as though Harry Sturz was a Byzantine priorist. He was not. At his death Harry Sturz was in

---

the most reliable form of the text, representing, more or less, what the New Testament authors wrote." See Rodgers, "Origins," 49. In one sense, then, it would probably not be incorrect to call reasoned eclecticism the "Alexandrian priority" position. (One well-known rigorous eclectic once told me that this proclivity to prefer the Alexandrian text type is due to the "hypnotic effect of Aleph and B.")

15. Sheffield Academic Press, 1997.

the process of editing his own edition of the Greek New Testament based on his working hypothesis that the Byzantine text was not edited in the Wescott-Hort sense and that it was an early and independent witness to the text of the New Testament. He called his work *The Second Century Greek New Testament*. In it he argued that the readings of all the text types push back into the second century. In this process he did not, I repeat *did not*, give preferential treatment to the Byzantine text, even though it was the one text type that least often stood alone in places of variation. This fact, however, was no argument for Byzantine priority in Sturz's mind. I must emphasize this point because Sturz has often been made into a defender of Byzantine priority. Again, nothing could be further from the truth.

In the second place, Sturz believed that the internal evidence played a very important role, if only a confirmatory one, in the field of New Testament textual criticism. Based on several conversations that I had with Professor Sturz, I believe his reticence to place too much emphasis on internal evidence was due to his concern about its inherent subjectivity and lack of perspicacity. I have already illustrated this from the text of Matt 5:22. Another example is one that was discussed at the Clearview Apologetics Conference, namely the text of Mark 1:2. Here the original reading is either "in Isaiah the prophet" (so most printed editions of the Greek New Testament as well as the majority of modern English translations) or "in the prophets" (so the KJV and NKJV). Generally speaking, reasoned eclectics will examine the internal evidence and conclude that the reading "in Isaiah the prophet" is vastly superior to "in the prophets" because in what follows there are actually *two* Old Testament quotations, not one. Both Isaiah and Malachi are quoted by Mark. The implication is obvious. A scribe, believing that more than one prophet was being quoted, invented the reading "in the prophets."

How do Byzantine priorists answer this question? At the conference, Maurice Robinson noted that one could still argue that "in the prophets" was original and was changed to "in Isaiah the prophet" because (in his opinion) there are not two quotations but only one quotation (Isaiah) and one allusion (Malachi). A look at the LXX of both texts indicates that this is a possibility. What would I say to all this? I agree with Robinson that the internal evidence is not as unambiguous as we might like to make it, though in my opinion it does seem that "in the prophets" is more likely to be secondary here due to an attempt to "correct" the text. But my preference for "in Isaiah the prophet" is based on the eternal evidence: this reading is found in two text types (Alexandrian and Western) as opposed to only one (Byzantine). Once again, the external evidence is probative: "in Isaiah the prophet" is original. The internal evidence then comes along and adds its *nihil obstat*.

SUMMARY AND CONCLUSION

Let me now attempt to summarize what I believe to be the most reasonable approach to take when trying to resolve places of textual variation in the New Testament. Because of space limitations, bullet points will have to suffice:

- No individual Greek manuscript can be equated with the original text of the New Testament.

- No single group of manuscripts or text types can be equated with the original text of the New Testament.

- No single printed edition of the Greek New Testament can be equated with the original text of the New Testament.

- No single English translation can be equated with the original text of the New Testament.

- All things being equal, readings that enjoy the support of the majority of text types are more likely to be original than not.[16]

- Internal evidence plays a crucial though subordinate role in determining the original text.

16. Again, Sturz himself did not insist that a consensus reading was necessarily the original reading. This, however, seems to me to be a clear inference of Sturz's work.

- Like rigorous eclecticism, the Sturzian approach eschews the unwarranted preference for any text type. Unlike rigorous eclecticism, the Sturzian approach regards the external evidence as probative and the internal evidence as (only) corroborative.

- Like reasoned eclecticism, the Sturzian approach takes both external and internal evidence into account. Unlike reasoned eclecticism, the Sturzian approach gives pride of place to the external evidence.

- Like Byzantine priority, the Sturzian position esteems the Byzantine text very highly. Unlike Byzantine priority, the Sturzian position does not give primacy of place to the Byzantine text.

I should finally like to make a completely anecdotal observation. In my personal experience, and in the several books and essays I have published on New Testament textual criticism, I have consistently found the Byzantine text to least often stand alone in places of variation. To me, this speaks of its good quality. Moreover, in every passage I have personally examined, I have found the internal evidence to corroborate and not contradict the conclusion I reached on the basis of the external evidence. Of course, this is more than the "general consensus of scholarship" can concede.

In the end, when it comes to the two thousand or so major textual variants in the Greek New Testament, I would argue that the original reading is indeed to be found in our printed Greek New Testaments as well as in our major English Bible translations. The only question is: Is the original reading printed in the text or in the apparatus? It is this question that makes textual criticism such an important and fascinating field of study.

CONCLUSION

ABIDAN PAUL SHAH AND DAVID ALAN BLACK

IN 2007, ELDON EPP summarized the new trend in New Testament
Textual Criticism as follows:

> (1) to move scholars away from thinking of the text as a
> single line of 'correct' or assured text, or (worse) as the
> complete or exclusive text of the New Testament, and
> (2) to allow readers to grasp visually the several possi-
> bilities in a variation unit so as to gain insight into the
> underlying narratives—to hear the differing voices that
> the several readings present. In this way, variants are
> confronted directly and they alert the user, for example,
> to Christological notions that did not triumph in early
> Christianity (so Ehrman), to ethical and worship issues
> that were matters of debate and of edification (so Parker),
> and to an array of varying perceptions, interpretations,
> and viewpoints preserved or presented by scribes.[1]

Unfortunately, this is no longer just a prognostication. It has become the mainstream definition of the discipline. Lack of a settled
original text only leads to lack of a settled biblical theology which
only leads to uncertain Christian doctrines and practice.

Thankfully, there are still many who continue to practice a
scientific approach to retrieving the original text of the New Testament, albeit from different starting points and assumptions regarding textual history. They are reputable scholars with academic
credentials who hold to the inspiration and inerrancy of the New

---

1. Epp, "Variants," 301.

Testament scriptures, as do the contributors to this book. Our prayer and hope is that in every generation there will be fresh voices from the academy, pulpit, and pew who will continue to marshal the search for the original text of the New Testament.

Bibliography

Aland, Barbara. "Kriterien zur Beurteilung kleinerer Papyrusfragmente des Neuen Testaments." In *New Testament Textual Criticism and Exegesis: Festschrift J. Delobel,* edited by Adelbert Denaux, 1–13. *Bibliotheca Ephemeridum Theologicarum Lovaniensium* 161. Leuven: Leuven University Press, 2002.

———. "Der textkritische und textgeschichtliche Nutzen früher Papyri, demonstriert am Johannesevangelium." In *Recent Developments in Textual Criticism: New Testament, Other Early Christian and Jewish Literature,* edited by Wim Weren and Dietrich-Alex Koch, 19–38. *Studies in Theology and Religion* 8. Assen, Netherlands: Royal Van Gorcum, 2003.

———. "New Testament Textual Research, its Methods and its Goals." In *Translating* the *New Testament: Text, Translation, Theology,* edited by Stanley E. Porter and Mark Boda, 13–26. *McMaster New Testament Studies.* Grand Rapids: Eerdmans, 2009.

———. "The Significance of the Chester Beatty Papyri in Early Church History." In *The Earliest Gospels: The Origins and Transmission of the Earliest Christian Gospels—The Contribution of the Chester Beatty Gospel Codex P45,* edited by Charles Horton, 108–21. *Journal for the Study of the New Testament Supplement Series* 258. London: T. & T. Clark, 2004.

Aland, Kurt, and Barbara Aland. *The Text of the New Testament: An Introduction to the Critical Editions and to the Theory and Practice of Modern Textual Criticism.* Translated by Erroll F. Rhodes. 2nd rev. and enl. ed. Grand Rapids: Eerdmans, 1989.

Bahnsen, Greg L. "The Inerrancy of the Autographa." In *Inerrancy,* edited by Norman Geisler, 151–93. Grand Rapids: Zondervan, 1980.

Balla, Peter. "Evidence for an Early Christian Canon (Second and Third Century)." In *The Canon Debate,* edited by Lee Martin McDonald and James A. Sanders, 372–85. Peabody, MA: Hendrickson, 2002.

Barr, James. *Holy Scripture: Canon, Authority, Criticism.* Philadelphia: Westminster, 1983.

Bauer, Walter, Frederick W. Danker, W. F. Arndt, and F. W. Gingrich. *Greek-English Lexicon of the New Testament and Other Early Christian Literature.* 3rd ed. Chicago: University of Chicago Press, 2000.

Beers, Rudolf. *Ioannis Wyclif: de compositione hominis*. London: Trübner, 1884.

Black, David Alan. "Jesus on Anger: The Text of Matthew 5:22a Revisited." *Novum Testamentum* 30 (1988) 1–8.

———. "The Peculiarities of Ephesians and the Ephesian Address." *Grace Theological Journal* 2:1 (Spring 1981) 45–58.

———. ed., *Rethinking New Testament Textual Criticism*. Grand Rapids: Baker, 2002.

———. "The Text of John 3:13." *Grace Theological Journal* 6 (1985) 49–66.

Bruce, F. F. *Answers to Questions*. Grand Rapids: Zondervan, 1972.

Carroll, Scott. "Nazaroo." No longer available online.

Carson, D. A. *Jesus' Sermon on the Mount and His Confrontation with the World: An Exposition of Matthew 5-10*. Grand Rapids: Baker, 1987.

Clark, Kenneth W. "The Effect of Recent Textual Criticism upon New Testament Studies." In *The Background of the New Testament and its Eschatology* edited by W. D. Davies and D. Daube, 27–51. Cambridge: University Press, 1956.

———. "The Manuscripts of the Greek New Testament." In *New Testament Manuscript Studies: The Materials and the Making of a Critical Apparatus* edited by Merrill M. Parvis and Allen P. Wikgren, 1–24. Chicago: University Press, 1950.

———. Personal interview with Maurice A. Robinson. 3 May 1977.

———. "Today's Problems with the Critical Text of the New Testament." In *Transitions in Biblical Scholarship* edited by J. Coert Rylaarsdam, 157–69. *Essays in Divinity* 6. Chicago: University Press, 1968.

Clarke, Kent D. *Textual Optimism: A Critique of the United Bible Societies' Geek New Testament*. Sheffield: Sheffield Academic Press, 1997.

Colwell, Ernest Cadman. "Method in Locating a Newly Discovered Manuscript." In Studies in Methodology in Textual Criticism of the New Testament, edited by E. C. Colwell, 26–44. *New Testament Tools and Studies* 9. Leiden: Brill, 1969.

———. *What Is the Best New Testament?* Chicago: University of Chicago Press, 1952.

Cosaert, Carl P. *The Text of the Gospels in Clement of Alexandria*. In *New Testament in the Greek Fathers* 9. Atlanta: SBL, 2008.

Dahl, Nils A. "The Particularity of the Pauline Epistles as a Problem in the Ancient Church." In *Neotestamentica et Patristica: Freundesgabe Herrn Professor Dr. Oscar Cullmann zu Seinem 60. Geburtstag*, edited by W. C. van Unnik, 261–71. Leiden: Brill, 1962.

Ehrman, Bart D. *Forged: Writing in the Name of God—Why the Bible's Authors are Not Who We Think They Are*. New York: HarperOne, 2011.

———. *Misquoting Jesus: The Story behind Who Changed the Bible and Why*. New York: HarperCollins, 2005.

———. *The Orthodox Corruption of Scripture: The Effect of Early Christological Controversies on the Text of the New Testament*. Updated ed. Oxford: Oxford University Press, 2011.

Elliott, J. K. "The Case for Thoroughgoing Eclecticism." In *Rethinking New Testament Textual Criticism*, edited by David Alan Black, 101–24. Grand Rapids: Baker, 2002.

———, ed. *New Testament Textual Criticism, the Application of Thoroughgoing Principles: Essays on Manuscripts and Textual Variation. Supplements to Novum Testamentum* 137. Leiden: Brill, 2010.

Epp, Eldon J. "A Continuing Interlude in New Testament Textual Criticism?" *Harvard Theological Review* 73 (1980) 131–51.

———. "The Eclectic Method in New Testament Textual Criticism: Solution or Symptom?" In *Studies in the Theory and Method of New Testament Textual Criticism*, edited by Eldon J. Epp and Gordon D. Fee, 141–173. *Studies and Documents* 45. Grand Rapids: Eerdmans, 1993.

———. "The Multivalence of the Term 'Original Text' in New Testament Textual Criticism," *Harvard Theological Review* 92.3 (1999) 245–81.

———. "New Testament Textual Criticism in America: Requiem for a Discipline," *Journal of Biblical Literature* 98 (1979) 94–98.

———. "Textual Criticism," in *The New Testament and Its Modern Interpreters* edited by Douglas A. Knight, 75–106. Philadelphia: Fortress, 1989.

———. "The Twentieth-Century Interlude in New Testament Textual Criticism," *Journal of Biblical Literature* 93 (1974) 386–414.

Erickson, Millard J. *Christian Theology*, 2nd ed. Grand Rapids: Baker, 1998.

Eusebius. *Ecclesiastical History*. Translated by C. F. Cruse. *Eusebius' Ecclesiastical History*, Complete and Unabridged, New Updated Edition. Peabody, MA: Hendrickson, 1998.

Fee, Gordon. "Rigorous or Reasoned Eclecticism—Which?" In *Studies in the New Testament Language and Text: Essays in Honour of George D. Kilpatrick on the Occasion of His Sixty-Fifth Birthday*, edited by J. K. Elliott, 174–197. Leiden: Brill, 1976; repr. in Eldon J. Epp and Gordon D. Fee, *Studies in the Theory and Method of New Testament Textual Criticism, Studies and Documents* 45. Grand Rapids: Eerdmans, 1993.

Feinberg, Paul. "The Meaning of Inerrancy." In *Inerrancy*, edited by Norman L. Geisler, 267–304. Grand Rapids, Mich.: Zondervan, 1980.

Foxe's Book of Martyrs. Edited by Marie Gentert King. Old Tappan, NJ: Spire, 1968.

Gamble, Harry Y. *The New Testament Canon: Its Making and Meaning*. Philadelphia: Fortress, 1985.

Grant, Robert M. "The Citation of Patristic Evidence in an Apparatus Criticus." In *Manuscript Studies* edited by Merrill M. Parvis and Allen P. Wikgren, 117–24. Chicago: University of Chicago Press, 1950.

Greenlee, J. Harold. *The Text of the New Testament: From Manuscript to Modern Edition*. Peabody, MA: Hendrickson, 2008.

Greetham, D. C. "A History of Textual Scholarship." In *The Cambridge Companion to Textual Scholarship*, edited by Neil Fraistat and Julia Flanders, 16–41. Cambridge: Cambridge University Press, 2013.

———. ed. *Scholarly Editing: A Guide to Research.* New York: Modern Language Association, 1995.

Gurry, Peter J. "The All-or-Nothing Problem with Byzantine Priority." *Evangelical Textual Criticism.* http://evangelicaltextualcriticism.blogspot.com/2019/01/the-all-or-nothing-problem-with.html.

———. *A Critical Examination of the Coherence-Based Genealogical Method in New Testament Textual Criticism.* New Testament Tools, Studies and Documents 55. Leiden: Brill, 2017.

———. "Ehrman's Definition of Textual Criticism." http://evangelical textualcriticism.blogspot.com/2022/10/ehrmans-definition-of-textual-criticism.html and https://ehrmanblog.org/the-strange-world-of-textual-criticism/.

———. "Inerrancy and the Initial Text." Presbyterion: Covenant Seminary Review 49:1 (Spring 2023) 54-67.

———. "Myths About Variants: Why some variants are insignificant and why some can't be ignored." In *Myths and Mistakes in New Testament Textual Criticism,* edited by Elijah Hixson and Peter J. Gurry, 191–210. Downers Grove, IL: IVP Academic, 2019.

———. "On Not Preferring the Shorter Reading: Matthew as a Test Case." In *Studies on the Intersection of Text, Paratext, and Reception: A Festschrift in Honor of Charles E. Hill,* edited by Gregory R. Lanier and J. Nicholas Reid, 122–41. *Text and Editions for New Testament Study* 15. Leiden: Brill, 2021.

———. "Text-Types and the Coherence-Based Genealogical Method." In *The Oxford Handbook of the Textual Criticism of the Bible,* edited by Sidnie White Crawford and Tommy Wasserman. Oxford: Oxford University Press, forthcoming.

———. "Textual Criticism." In *Dictionary of Paul and His Letters: A Compendium of Contemporary Biblical Scholarship,* edited by Scot McKnight, Lynn H. Cohick, and Nijay K. Gupta. Downers Grove, IL: InterVarsity, forthcoming.

———. "The Number of Variants in the Greek New Testament: A Proposed Estimate." *New Testament Studies* 62.1 (2016) 97–121.

Haines-Eitzen, Kim. *Guardians of Letters: Literacy, Power, and the Transmitters of Early Christian Literature.* New York: Oxford University Press, 2000.

Harris, R. Laird. *Inspiration and Canonicity of the Bible: An Historical and Exegetical Study.* Contemporary Evangelical Perspectives rev. ed. Grand Rapids: Zondervan, 1971.

Hodges, Zane Clark. "The Greek Text of the King James Version." *Bibliotheca Sacra* 125 (1968) 334–45.

———. "A Defense of the Majority Text." Dallas: Seminary Book Room, n.d.

Hodges, Zane Clark and David M. Hodges. "Appendix C: The Implications of Statistical Probability for the History of the Text." In *The Identity of the New Testament Text,* 4th ed. Wilbur N. Pickering, 263–74. Eugene OR: Wipf and Stock, 2014.

Hoehner, Harold. *Ephesians: An Exegetical Commentary.* Grand Rapids: Baker, 2002.

Holmes, Michael W. "From 'Original Text' to 'Initial Text': The Traditional Goal of New Testament Textual Criticism in Contemporary Discussion." In *The Text of the New Testament in Contemporary Research: Essays on the Status Quaestionis*, edited by Bart D. Ehrman and Michael W. Holmes, 637–88. *New Testament Tools, Studies, and Documents* 42. Leiden: Brill, 2013.

————. "Text and Transmission in the Second Century." In *The Reliability of the New Testament: Bart D. Ehrman and Daniel B. Wallace in Dialogue*, edited by Robert B. Stewart, 61–80. Minneapolis: Fortress, 2011.

Hort, Arthur Fenton. "Letter 'To the Rev. John Ellerton." In *Life and Letters of Fenton John Anthony Hort,* 2 vols. December 1851. London: Macmillan and Co., 1896, 1:211, 209–12

Housman, A. E. "The Application of Thought to Textual Criticism." http://rosetta.reltech.org/TC/extras/Housman-Thought.html.

Hills, Edward F. *The King James Version Defended*, 4th ed. Des Moines: Christian Research, 1984.

Imhof, Max. "Anhang zur Überlieferungsgeschichte der nichtchristlichen griechischen Literatur der römischen Kaizerzeit." In *Geschichte der Textüberlieferung der antiken und mittelalterlichen Literatur,* Band 1: Antikes und Mittelalterliches Buch- und Schriftwesen: Überlieferungsgeschichte der Antiken Literatur, edited by Herbert Hunger et al., Zürich: Atlantis, 1961.

Kilpatrick, George D. "Review of UBS3 and Metzger's Textual Commentary." *Theologische Literaturzeitung* 104:4 (1979) 260–70.

————. "Western Text and Original Text in Gospels and Acts." *The Journal of Theological Studies,* 44.173/174 (1943) 24–36.

Kloha, Jeffrey J. "A Textual Commentary on Paul's First Epistle to the Corinthians." PhD diss., University of Leeds, 2006.

Knust, Jennifer Wright. "In Pursuit of a Singular Text: New Testament Textual Criticism and the Desire for the True Original." *Religion Compass* 2.2 (2008) 180–94.

Lagrange, M.-J. *Introduction a l'étude du nouveau testament: deuxième partie: Critique textuelle II: la critique rationnelle*, 2nd ed. Paris: Lecoffre, 1935.

Lake, Kirsopp and Silva Lake. "The Byzantine Text of the Gospels." In *Mémorial Lagrange*, edited by L.-H Vincent, 251–58. Cinquantenaire de L'École Biblique et Archéologique Française de Jérusalem. Paris: J. Gabalda et Cie, 1940.

Landon, Charles. *A Text-Critical Study of the Epistle of Jude. Journal for the Study of the New Testament Supplement Series* 135. Sheffield: Sheffield Academic, 1996.

Larsen, Matthew David. *Gospels Before the Book.* New York: Oxford University Press, 2018.

———. "Accidental Publication, Unfinished Texts and the Traditional Goals of New Testament Textual Criticism." *Journal for the Study of the New Testament* 39.4 (2017) 362–87.

McKnight, Scot. *The Blue Parakeet: Rethinking How You Read the Bible*, rev. ed., Grand Rapids: Zondervan, 2016.

Mink, Gerd. "Problems of a Highly Contaminated Tradition, the New Testament: Stemmata of Variants as a Source of a Genealogy for Witnesses." In *Studies in Stemmatology II*, edited by Pieter Th. Van Reenen, A. A. den Hollander, and Margot van Mulken, 13–86. Amsterdam: John Benjamins Publishing, 2004.

Metzger, Bruce M. *The Text of the New Testament: Its Transmission, Corruption, and Restoration*, 1st ed. Oxford: Oxford University Press, 1964.

———. *A Textual Commentary on the Greek New Testament.* 2nd ed. Stuttgart: Deutsche Bibelgesellschaft, 1994.

Metzger, Bruce M. and Bart D. Ehrman. *The Text of the New Testament: Its Transmission, Corruption, and Restoration*, 4th ed. Oxford: Oxford University Press, 2005.

Miller, Edward, *The Present State of the Textual Controversy respecting the Holy Gospels.* Printed for Private Circulation, 1898.

Mitchell, Timothy N. "Myths about Autographs: What They Were and How Long They May Have Survived." In *Myths and Mistakes in New Testament Textual Criticism*, edited by Elijah Hixson and Peter J. Gurry, 26–47. Downers Grove, IL: IVP Academic, 2019.

Mohler, Albert R. "When the Bible speaks, God speaks: The classic doctrine of biblical inerrancy." In *Five Views on Biblical Inerrancy*, edited by James R. A. Merrick and Stephen M. Garrett, 29–58. Grand Rapids: Zondervan, 2013.

Moyise, Steve. "Composite Citations in the Gospel of Mark." In *Composite Citations in Antiquity, Volume 2: New Testament Uses*, edited by Sean A. Adams and Seth E. Ehorn, 16–33. London: Bloomsbury/T&T Clark, 2018.

O'Neill, J. C. "The Rules followed by the Editors of the Text found in the Codex Vaticanus." *Novum Testamentum* 35 (1989) 219–28.

Origen, *Against Celsus*. Translated by Alexander Roberts, James Donaldson, and A. Cleveland Coxe. *The Ante-Nicene Fathers: Translations of the Writings of the Fathers down to AD 325*. Volume 4. Buffalo, NY: The Christian Literature Publishing Company, 1885.

Packer, James I. "Text Criticism and Inerrancy." *Christianity Today* 46.11 (2002) 102.

Parker, David C. *The Living Text of the Gospels*. Cambridge: Cambridge University Press, 1997.

Parkes, M. B. *Pause and Effect: An Introduction to the History of Punctuation in the West*. Berkley: University of California Press, 1993.

Pierpont, William G. "Textual Criticism." Unpublished papers, ca. 1975-1980
———. unpublished document found among his many files.

Porter, Calvin L. "A Textual Analysis of the Earliest Manuscripts of the Gospel of John." PhD diss., Duke University, 1961.

Reilly, Ignatius J. *Blood on their Hands: The Crime of it All. A Study of Some Selected Abuses in Sixteenth-century Europe,* Monograph, 2pp, edited by J. K. Toole. Rare Book Room, Howard-Tilton Memorial Library, New Orleans: Tulane University, 1950.

Renehan, Robert. *Greek Textual Criticism: A Reader.* Loeb Classical Monographs, Cambridge: Harvard University Press, 1969.

Roberts, Donaldson, et al. eds. *The Ante-Nicene Fathers: Translations of the Writings of the Fathers down to AD 325.* Volume 5. Buffalo, NY: The Christian Literature Publishing Company, 1886.

Robertson, A. T. *The Minister and His Greek New Testament.* New York: George H. Duran Co., 1923.

Robinson, Maurice A. "*De facto* Conjecture in the Main Text of NA27: A Further Consideration." Paper presented to the Evangelical Theological Society, 64th Annual Meeting. November 2012, Milwaukee, Wisconsin.

———. "The Byzantine-Priority Perspective Regarding the Recognition of Autograph Originality." Paper presented at the "Making Christ Reasonable" conference at Clearview Church in Henderson, NC on September 24, 2022.

———. "The Integrity of the Early New Testament Text: A Collation-Based Comparison Utilizing the Papyri of the Second and Third Centuries." Paper presented at the Annual Meeting of the Evangelical Theological Society, Valley Forge, PA, 2005.

———. "'It's All About Variants'—unless 'No Longer Written.'" In *Getting into the Text: New Testament: Essays in Honor of David Alan Black* edited by Daniel L. Akin and Thomas W. Hudgins, 116–53. Eugene OR: Pickwick, 2017.

———. "New Testament Textual Criticism: The Case for Byzantine Priority." *TC: A Journal of Biblical Textual Criticism* 6 (2001) 11–23.

———. "The Recensional Nature of the Alexandrian Text-Type: A Response to Selected Criticisms of the Byzantine-Priority Theory." *Faith and Mission* 11:1 (1993) 46–74,

———. "Rule 9, Isolated Variants, and the 'Test-Tube' Nature of the NA27/UBS4 Text." In *Translating the New Testament Text: Text, Translation, Theology,* edited by Stanley E. Porter and Mark J. Boda, 27–61. Grand Rapids: Eerdmans, 2009.

Robinson, Maurice A. and William G. Pierpont. *The New Testament in the Original Greek: Byzantine Textform 2018.* Nürnberg: VTR, 2018.

Rodgers, Peter R. "The Origins of the Alexandrian Text of the New Testament." *Filología Neotestamentaria* 35 (2022) 49–53.

Scrivener, Frederick Henry Ambrose. *A Full and Exact Collation of about Twenty Greek Manuscripts of the Holy Gospels . . . with a Critical Introduction.* Cambridge: Cambridge University Press, 1853.

————. *A Plain Introduction to the Criticism of the New Testament for the Use of Biblical Students*, 4th ed. Edited by Edward Miller. London: George Bell, 1894.

Sheffield, Jonathan. "A James White Halloween Special: The Textual Frankenstein of Modern Critical Text Theory." YouTube video. 21:01. https://youtu.be/tbJ33bxBnWA.

Smith, D. Moody. "When did the Gospels become Scripture?" *Journal of Biblical Literature* 119/1 (2000) 3–20.

Shah, Abidan Paul. *Changing the Goalpost of New Testament Textual Criticism.* Eugene, OR: Wipf and Stock, 2020.

Strouse, Susan M. "Magnificat! Dismantling patriarchy in the world's religions." *Dismantling Patriarchy.* https://dismantlingpatriarchy753717292.blog/author/smstrouse/.

Sturz, Harry A. *The Byzantine Text-Type & New Testament Textual Criticism.* Cantonment, FL: Energion, 2022.

————. *The Byzantine Text-Type & New Testament Textual Criticism.* Nashville: Thomas Nelson, 1984.

————. *The Second Century Greek New Testament: Matthew.* La Mirada CA: Biola College Book Store, 1973.

Theophilos, Michael P. "An Assessment of the Authenticity of John 9:38-39a." *Australian Journal of Theology* 19:1 (2012) 73–85.

Tischendorf, Constantine. *The New Testament: The Authorised English Version; With Introduction, And Various Readings from the Three Most Celebrated Manuscripts of the Original Greek Text.* Tauchnitz Edition 1000. Leipzig: Bernhard Tauchnitz, 1869.

Tuchman, Barbara W. *A Distant Mirror: The Calamitous 14th Century.* New York: Alfred A. Knopf, 1978.

Turner, C. H. "Marcan Usage: Notes, Critical and Exegetical, on the Second Gospel: VII. Particles (Continued)." *The Journal of Theological Studies* 28.109 (1926) 9–30.

Vaganay, Léon. *An Introduction to the Textual Criticism of the New Testament.* Translated by B. V. Miller. London: Sands, 1937.

Victor, Ulrich. "Textkritischer Kommentar zu ausgewählten Stellen des Lukas- und des Johannesevangeliums." *Novum Testamentum* 51 (2009) 30–77.

Von Soden, Hermann. *Die Schriften des Neuen Testaments in ihrer ältesten erreichbaren Textgestalt.* 2 vols. Göttingen: Vandenhoeck und Ruprecht, 1911-13.

Wachtel, Klaus. "Conclusion." In *The Textual History of the Greek New Testament: Changing Views in Contemporary Research*, edited by Klaus Wachtel and Michael W. Holmes, 217–26. *Text-Critical Studies* 8 Atlanta: SBL, 2011.

————. "A Discussion of Several Variant Passages in the Letters of Peter," paper presented at the SNTS annual meeting, Tel Aviv, Israel, August 2000.

Wachtel, Klaus and Michael W. Holmes. "Introduction." In *The Textual History of the Greek New Testament: Changing Views in Contemporary Research*, edited by Klaus Wachtel and Michael W. Holmes, 1–12. *Text-Critical Studies* 8. Atlanta: SBL, 2011.

Wasserman, Tommy. "Textual Criticism." In *The Dictionary of the Bible and Ancient Media*, edited by Tom Thatcher et al, 407–17. London: T&T Clark, 2017.

Watts, Rikki E. *Isaiah's New Exodus in Mark*. Biblical Studies Library. Grand Rapids: Baker, 2012.

West, Logan. "An Inadequate View of God's Providence regarding Manuscripts of the NT." #254. https://www.puritanboard.com/threads/an-inadequate-view-of-gods-providence-regarding-manuscripts-of-the-nt.109376/page-2.

Westcott, Brooke Foss. "Collect for a devout reverence of God's Word." In Arthur Westcott, *Life and Letters of Brooke Foss Westcott.* 2 vols. London: Macmillan, 1903.

Westcott, Brooke Foss and Fenton John Anthony Hort. *New Testament in the Original Greek,* London: Macmillan, 1882.

Whitney, S. W. *The Revisers' Greek Text: A Critical Examination of Certain Readings, Textual and Marginal, in the Original Greek of the New Testament adopted by the late Anglo-American Revisers.* 2 vols. Boston: Silver, Burdett and Co., 1892.

Will, George F. *Statecraft as Soulcraft: What Government Does.* New York: Simon and Schuster, 1983.

Zuntz, Günther. *The Text of the Epistles: A Disquisition upon the Corpus Paulinum.* Schweich Lectures. Oxford: Oxford University Press, 1953.

———. Personal interview with Maurice A. Robinson. 3 May 1977.

———. "Today's Problems with the Critical Text of the New Testament." In *Transitions in Biblical Scholarship* edited by J. Coert Rylaarsdam, 157–69. *Essays in Divinity* 6. Chicago: Chicago University Press, 1968.

www.ingramcontent.com/pod-product-compliance
Lightning Source LLC
Chambersburg PA
CBHW070738030726
47601CB00001B/57